FORTY ACRES AND STEEL MULES

"It is false to assume that share croppers and share tenants are humanly hopeless."

A SHARE-CROPPER FAMILY NEAR HAZELHURST, GEORGIA

"The South has more farm tenants and poorer tenants than any other section of the country."

MOVING DAY IN THE ARKANSAS COTTON LANDS

HERMAN CLARENCE NIXON

FORTY ACRES AND STEEL MULES

CHAPEL HILL
THE UNIVERSITY
OF NORTH CAROLINA
PRESS

MCMXXXVIII

COPYRIGHT, 1938, BY
THE UNIVERSITY OF NORTH CAROLINA PRESS

P.J.

Van Rees Press · New York

PREFACE

IN THIS STUDY I HAVE ATTEMPTED A FRESH AND INTEGRATED INTERPRETAtion of the rural South. However, the following pages may show a kinship at times with my former writings in this sphere of interest, with different magazine articles, with "Whither Southern Economy?" in *I'll Take My Stand* by twelve Southerners (Harper & Brothers, 1930), and with "The New South and the Old Crop" in *Essays in Honor of William E. Dodd,* edited by Avery Craven (University of Chicago Press, 1935). As a former student of his, I owe a certain influence to Ambassador Dodd, and that influence is in this book, distorted though it may seem to him. I am grateful to him for comments given me while this study was under way. There is not only kinship but discrepancy between the present study and my chapter in *I'll Take My Stand,* and I wish to anticipate any possible critic in making this point. I participated in the "agrarian" indictment of the American industrial system of the nineteen-twenties, but I seek a broader program of agricultural reconstruction than I read into the writings which have come from most members of that group since 1930. It should be said that what I have here written is by way neither of conformity nor of dissent. My ideas or observations must speak for themselves. I offer them for whatever merit they may have, relying on the country woman's dictum, "What I am, I am, and nobody can't make me no ammer."

This is a short book with only a moderate amount of statistical information. But I have sought to make it a discussion of a few big ideas, which

PREFACE

have a bearing on the South today and on contemporary rural trends. I have worried friends and colleagues, not so much with having them read passages and chapters, as with compulsory conversation on points which seemed important to me. Thanks and apologies are due especially to W. T. Couch, director of the University of North Carolina Press, Professor Mack Swearingen, of Tulane University, and Anne Trice Nixon, my wife.

The photographs come from the Division of Information of the Farm Security Administration. Their excellent quality is a consequence of the interest and oversight of Mr. Roy E. Stryker, chief of the Historical Section.

It might be mentioned that Mr. Couch and I originally had in mind a study of Southern farm villages, but further thought seemed to make it clear that farm tenancy, rural trade, local industries, and other factors should also be considered for a proper perspective. I have avowedly attempted to go beyond a diagnosis of the ills of the South and to give as much attention as possible to general and particular proposals for improvement. These suggestions are offered with a hope for constructive change under an enlightened leadership, a leadership devoted to applied democracy and economic democracy. I believe in that leadership and believe it is possible.

H. C. N.

CONTENTS

		PAGE
	Preface	v
Chapter I	A Hillbilly's View	3
II	Plains, Hills, and Farmers	7
III	Share Tenants and Croppers	17
IV	Merchants and Markets	28
V	Towns and Villages	38
VI	Farms for Farmers	48
VII	Villages for Villagers	61
VIII	Local Industries and Workshops	71
IX	Social Planning and Action	79
X	The South's Role in the Nation	90
	Selected Bibliography	97

FORTY ACRES AND STEEL MULES

CHAPTER ONE

A HILLBILLY'S VIEW

THIS BOOK IS A HILLBILLY'S VIEW OF THE SOUTH. IT UNDERTAKES TO present a picture of certain phases of Southern civilization and to suggest a few points for a program of reconstruction. It is not primarily a factual survey, though it makes use of pertinent facts which have been set forth by various writers and investigators. It has received impetus from my experiences as a student in a land grant college of the South and as a teacher of American history and government in a land grant college of the Middle West. It is an attempt to interpret the rural South and the village South in the light of the inevitable trends of the times. It is based partly on research, partly on general reading, and largely on direct observation. More important than research carried on with teaching in four different Southern institutions of higher learning was my research among human beings on an Alabama upland plantation over a period of two decades.

I was born in a farm house by the side of a road, opposite a postoffice which has been discontinued. One might say that I grew up behind the counter of a country store in which this postoffice was located. I handled mail and also wrote many letters for patrons who could not read and write, frequently using the dictated formula, "These few lines leave me well and hoping they will find you the same." I attended a church in the woods and heard many revival sermons. I learned about Frank and Jesse James from a colored plowman. I served for years as country correspondent for a county newspaper. I had an early ambition to join the ranks of "drummers," who seemed so well travelled and full of stories. I vividly remember an unlettered tenant farmer for his native wit and humor. He was a good cotton grower but was tall and hated the task of cotton-picking. He said that sight of the first open boll gave him the backache. I have picked enough cotton to appreciate his comment.

The store in which I grew up served as commissary, office and general clearing-house for the plantation. It was a center from which I witnessed the evolution of farm methods from the use of oxen for deep plowing to the use of tractors. I observed the first and expanding use of two-mule cultivators by tenants of both races. I noted the change from "dropping corn" by hand to the use of mechanical corn planters. I saw the effects of tenancy and constant cropping on hillside fields. I saw good farm lands brought into larger units of ownership, with greater difficulties for actual farmers seeking to acquire relatively small holdings. I observed the removal from the community of many active young persons, and I myself migrated several years ago. In my boyhood the community sent migrants to farm lands of Texas and Oklahoma. Subsequently it has fed population more conspicuously to urban centers.

There are a few important impressions which have stuck in my memory since my early days in the country store. One is of the rather wide margin of "time" or credit prices as compared with the prices of merchandise sold for cash. Another concerns the difficulty and the importance of the merchant's keeping the tenant's account within bounds as measured by the values of the growing crop. One particular tenant, whose landlord wished us to watch him against overtrading, adopted the policy of prefacing every purchase with the remark that he was "entirely out" of the sort of goods he was about to buy, even when asking one day for a pair of trousers. Somewhat later I became impressed by the prevalence of the one-crop policy among tenants and croppers as a line of least resistance for both tenant and landlord. I know from disillusioning experience how difficult it is to prevail upon share croppers to practice effective diversification. The seasonal enforced idleness and the lack of community life among one-crop tenants have been vividly etched upon my mind. There

A HILLBILLY'S VIEW

have been many other observations which have a bearing on the study I am presenting.

I learned something about tenancy, farm management and balanced agriculture during the depression. As a director of the Louisiana Rural Rehabilitation Corporation I saw farm problems from the relief administration angle. I also got another slant. About ten years ago the plantation with which my life has been associated became part of an unencumbered estate involving minor heirs, whose interest could not be jeopardized by lien or mortgage. As senior heir I inherited the task of directing the policy of the estate and keeping it in operation on a cash basis. We reduced cash needs and risks by cutting down cotton acreage and increasing other crops before the AAA came into the picture and paid us for doing what we had been doing. The farming group included tenants and members of the owning class, a total of fifteen families. The tenants have managed to break even annually or end the year slightly ahead of the game, whether Coolidge, Hoover or Roosevelt was in the White House. They stayed off the relief rolls, and neither CWA nor PWA activities pulled them away from plantation work. Keeping the plantation out of debt has tended to keep the tenants out of debt. Repairs and plantation works, with cash wages, have minimized idleness and stimulated tenant morale. The farm policy has paid little in the way of net dividends, has not met the expectations of the absentee owners, and can not be considered permanent. The permanent savings of the tenants have been small. Both profit and loss have been conspicuous for their absence. But all on the land have had a living, the land has been improved, and the tenant turnover has been reduced to about one in fifteen per annum. Immunity from financial abuse or speculation, a certain amount of practical coöperation, and a limitation on the returns to landlords have caused the farmers on these lands to fare better than isolated small farmers, whether tenants or owners, in the general community. This experiment convinces me that the South must face the problem of absentee ownership but not with the individualistic remedy of "forty acres and a mule."

Forty acres and a mule no longer offer an adequate solution for the farm ills of the South. They might have worked effectively when they were

FORTY ACRES AND STEEL MULES

first suggested three score and ten years ago, but they are not enough now. Even a moderately efficient share cropper in the cotton country today requires two mules and substantial equipment to make a go of farming. More mechanization is applicable in particular sub-regions than in others, and more intensive farming may be necessary in certain fertile areas not suited to long furrows and machine cultivation. Passing from the mechanical to the business aspects of farming, it is again to be noted that independent small tracts are inadequate except in special cases or on some coöperative basis. The tractor, which is a reality on many Southern farms, and the cotton-picker, which may soon be a reality in cotton fields, suggest important readjustments in the agricultural economy of this region. The mule in the flesh must be adjusted to the steel mule, and both must be subordinated to the service of rural society. No little economic and political action is necessary to save the day for the mass of Southern farmers. More education and more statesmanship are imperative.

FSA *Rothstein*

An Alabama tenant farmer. "He needs two mules and substantial equipment to make a go of farming in the cotton country today."

FSA *Mydan*

The blacksmith shop survives in a region using more mule flesh for plow power than any other part of the country.

FSA *Lange*

"The steel mule threatens to plow the small farmer under." This ex-tenant in Mississippi works (about 190 days out of 365) for wages.

FSA *Rothstein*

Tenant farmer with the mule supplied by the Resettlement Administration, Tupelo Homesteads, Mississippi.

FSA *Lange*

"The mule in the flesh must be adjusted to the steel mule, and both must be subordinated to the service of rural society."

FSA *Lange*

"The steel mule demands more than forty acres." The Aldridge Plantation near Leland, Mississippi.

A Cajan family in Washington County, Alabama.

An Alabama tenant farmer's wife and some of her children.

Descendants of the Pettway Plantation slaves, Gee's Bend, Alabama.

"Large families often make out with two or three rooms."

A tenant farmer with part of his family, Walker County, Alabama.

Children of a Negro share cropper, near West Memphis, Arkansas.

"POPULATION HAS BEEN THE MOST CONSISTENT SURPLUS CROP OF THE SOUTH."

CHAPTER TWO

PLAINS, HILLS, AND FARMERS

THE ROAR OF TRACTORS HAS BEEN REPLACING THE SOUND OF NEGRO SONGS here and there on Southern farms in the twentieth century. Those steel mules and other mechanical farm implements are especially in vogue on the Texas plains, where one may "plow a furrow a mile long" and consider farming a "sedentary occupation." Tractor farmers are giving small farmers keen competition for control of the lands in that state. It is estimated that half a million Texas farm workers, with their labor-saving machinery, produce as much cotton as several million workers in India. Steel mules have replaced or supplemented the more natural and stubborn variety on not a few farms of the Southeast, particularly in the less hilly areas. However, the farmers of the South use more mule flesh for plow power than any other region. There are many farms which are too small or too rough and hilly for any great use of elaborate machinery. Many small farmers are too poor to buy machinery, and there are farmers who could not use it if they had it. There are spots of land which would not yield sufficient returns to pay for mechanical cultivation.

The steel mule demands more than forty acres. It demands, moreover, fairly good acres and a degree of human competence to justify its existence in agriculture. It harmonizes neither with individualistic, small-scale proprietary farming nor with the South's traditional combination of absentee farm ownership and low-type share tenancy. Highly mechanized farming and inefficient plantation business methods do not go together.

FORTY ACRES AND STEEL MULES

Mechanization of agriculture suggests large-scale operation, which, in turn, suggests farming by wealthy individuals, by corporations, or by co-operative enterprise. The individual farmer with only forty acres and a mule can not compete, either as tenant or owner, with mechanized large-scale production of major staples without lowering his standard of living. The steel mule ever threatens to plow him under.

The eastern section of the cotton belt, with boll weevil troubles and Texas competition, had a mixture of agricultural reform and exodus of farmers in the fabulous twenties. In the depression days of the thirties it experienced a back-to-the-poor-land movement and as acute a problem of poverty as was known in Western Europe or America. The South of poverty is really the Southeast, for Texas and Oklahoma, though cotton states, are excluded from the South by many tests of economy and culture. These two states belong to the West on many counts rather than to the less wealthy South, though they are by no means free from rural poverty. The plains and hills of the South, with a mixture of modern and antiquated methods of farming, have revealed an agriculture which has many of the human insecurities of industry plus other risks not known to industry. This region has certain insecurities of agriculture not common to other farm areas.

The South today, especially the Southeast, is essentially a land of hillbillies and other ruralites, whose chief contact with the commerce and culture of the world is through hick towns. There are open spaces between the towns, and there are valleys between the hills, which grade downward from mountains to rolling plains, with the whole topography finally fading into coastal sands or delta bottoms.

It is natural that "hillbilly" should be a prevalent term in the Southeast. Along with the plains and plains people of the Southwest, the hill sections and the hill persons have constituted the most dynamic items in the civilization south of the Potomac since slavery. As decisive factors in human geography, the hills and mountains of Dixie can hardly be overestimated. More accessible or more penetrable for human life than the Western ranges, they are salubrious and tree-covered. They can supply tall tales and tall men. Unlike the Himalayas or the American

PLAINS, HILLS, AND FARMERS

Rockies, they lack those excessively rugged features which seem to "paralyze the mind." They release a heavy rainfall and feed a legion of streams and navigable rivers. These rain-river factors made possible a commercial agriculture between mountain and coast with the beginnings of human settlements, so that the plantation economy could develop step by step with a receding frontier. The Appalachians indirectly stimulated, guided and limited the spread of the slavery-plantation system; they constituted a dividing wedge against the solidarity of Southern interest and effort in the Civil War; and they furnished the basis and backbone of the Southern industrial revolution after that war. They brought the hillbillies to the forefront. They give variety to farm problems and cotton problems.

The up-country has really been important in Southern life since the middle of the colonial era of Virginia. But prior to 1860 it yielded social leadership to a lowland aristocracy. The low-country has contributed much to the tone and tradition of Southern life. When the South looks at its past it looks at a charming "agrarian way of life," which was made possible by rivers and river bottoms, a commercial agriculture, and the labor of human slaves. This view, which is available through the eyes of foreign travellers, overlooks the fact that the charming life was at no time the privilege of more than a few thousand families, while slaves, "poor whites," yeomen farmers and small slaveowners constituted the millions of the population and furnished the concealed reality of Southern economy.

The seeming stability of the social structure of the old South was due to the shifting conditions resulting from a comparative abundance of new lands for the spread of slavery and cotton culture. Southern hillbillies did not seek the end of the slaveocracy, for it was expanding and recruiting membership from the hills. Nonslaveowners expected to become small slaveowners, and small slaveowners expected to become large ones. More slaves also meant more lands. Jefferson Davis himself was an example of an upward climb into a land-and-slavery aristocracy whose demand for expansion he militantly supported. The hope and flavor of society came from the top, which also handed down to posterity a body of traditions and an extreme distaste for criticism or analysis of labor relations.

Whatever the values of the civilization of the ante-bellum South, that civilization was insecure. It was socially too much like that of Russia before the World War and sure to fall sooner or later. It was characterized by a dynamic growth of population, demanding a parallel expansion of economic activity. This demand was met between 1830 and 1860 in the same way a similar demand was met between 1865 and 1930, through an expansion of cotton production, supplemented by an industrial expansion particularly in the last decade of the period. The limits to cotton acreage expansion were limits to slavery, and concern over this fact gave Southern leaders of the fifties the jitters. J. D. B. De Bow, the ante-bellum champion of Southern industrialism, predicted the problem of a surplus slave population and urged that it be met by an expansion of factories and railroads, by "an industrial revolution in the South." Industrial expansion would absorb surplus slave labor released from the farms. But this idea was opposed by Southerners who knew or feared that an industrial revolution would terminate slavery. Had De Bow included a forecast of the growth of the white population, he would have been more nearly correct as an observer of the uneven relationship between Southern population and Southern economy.

Population has been the most consistent surplus crop of the South, and the older parts of the region have been exporting such a surplus for a hundred years. It has cost this section many hundred millions of dollars to rear and educate its net export of population in the twentieth century. A. P. Brigham, the geographer, thirty years ago observed that "a hundred millions of people could live within the valleys and on the wide plains of the old Confederacy." Much more has been done in the region of the Confederacy toward producing a hundred million people than toward providing a decent living for a fraction of that number. The census of 1930 showed a net export of more than three million population from the South. Population increase and shiftings constitute the most dynamic set of Southern problems.

The South is a land of farms and farmers. It contains about half the

"All God's chillun got shoes."   "White girls work in bare feet in cottonfields."

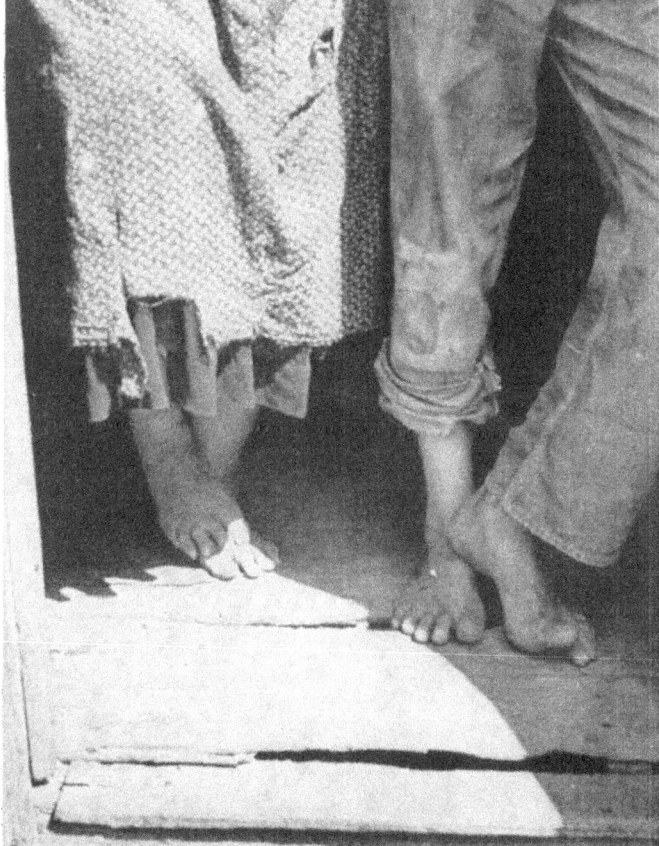

Bare feet in Oklahoma.   A Negro share cropper and his wife in Mississippi.

"THE SOUTH DOES NOT LEAD THE NATION IN THE PURCHASE AND WEARING OF SHOES."

On the Alexander Plantation, Pulaski County, Arkansas.

"The sight of the first cotton boll gave her a backache."

These cotton hoers in the Mississippi Delta work from 6:00 A.M. to 6:00 P.M. for $1.00.

Arkansas children chopping cotton.

The man with a hoe and a woman with hers.

EXCESSIVE RURALISM HAS CAUSED AN UNUSUAL AMOUNT OF LABOR OF WOMEN AND CHILDREN.

PLAINS, HILLS, AND FARMERS

farmers of the country, and, therefore, a proportionately small share of the nation's industrial population. The farm population of any one of half a dozen Southern states outnumbers by scores of thousands that of the largest farm state of the North. To appraise the South is to appraise farmers, whether for the art of living or for the lack of a living. Even Southern Indians, prior to their removal, had developed agricultural habits to an extent not commonly attained by their Northern kindred. Agricultural development was particularly true of the lowland Creeks and the upland Cherokees.

Geographic factors in the South have favored an agricultural exploitation on a rather easy-going basis and as a policy of least resistance. Most of the region receives an annual rainfall of more than fifty inches and offers a growing season of more than two hundred frostless nights, the growing time required for cotton. Incidentally it is the long summer rather than the extremely hot summer which characterizes the South as a whole and tends to moderate the tempo of human activity. The soil of the region, which escaped the glacial influences, has generally been found softer and easier to clear and break up, as well as to cultivate, than much of that of the rest of the country, especially of New England. A wide variety of soil qualities is found in the South. There are coastal plains which were made partly by deposits from a receding sea. This land in spots has a productivity sufficient only for "piney woods" unless tons of fertilizer be used, as in Florida, for an agricultural capture of the climate. There are level stretches of high fertility, especially the black belt of Alabama, the delta of the Mississippi, and the "black waxie" plains of Texas, while the Virginia "tidewater" was rich enough to cradle an aristocracy. The rule of variety applies equally to the soil of the uplands. The limestone valleys of such inland rivers as the Tennessee and the Cumberland deserve mention for sustained productivity. The mountains contain rich coves as well as marginal areas and government lands which man has never sought as a free gift.

The comparatively soft soil, the many large and small hills, the heavy rainfall without deep freezes, the staple crops which require abundant plant food and frequent plowing—these factors have combined to effect much more soil exhaustion and erosion in the South than has been true elsewhere in America. They must be taken into account in any explanation of the old and continuous Southern practice of abandoning old lands for new. They have forced folk movements.

The distinctive crops of the Southland, though heavy taxers of the soil, have an unusual commercial value in proportion to weight and bulk. Cotton, tobacco, sugar, rice, or citrus fruits can bear a higher traffic cost than corn, wheat, oats, or even livestock. Corn in olden days had to be turned into spirituous liquid before it could be hauled overland to market as far as could cotton. On the other hand, the Southern agricultural staples have always been in reach of relatively cheap transportation. A network of river traffic preceded the coming of railroads and touched seaports, which were not excessively distant from farm communities of the crescent-shaped South. Agriculture brought railroads for supplementary purposes into much of the South, while railroads had to take agriculture into much of the West.

The distinctive crops of the South are commodities which must immediately enter into the channels of commerce, for they can not be consumed to any appreciable degree on the producing farm or plantation. A grain farmer of the North or West has a product to eat, feed and sell, and necessity or direct expectation of profit may impel him to practice an agricultural program with a scientific and economic balance. He may, for instance, use hogs as "freight condensers" for corn. But a cotton farmer, a tobacco farmer, or a sugar farmer can neither consume his product nor utilize it in the production of other items for sale. He produces for a world market, a market which is complicated and which he does not understand. He is a part of the game of commerce, but his role in this game is the extremely easy function of direct selling for a price fixed by others, by fate.

The economy of Southern agriculture is, for the farmer, a seemingly simple economy, suggesting minimum requirements of private intelligence or public planning. Cotton, the chief crop, always sells for something and can be produced by almost any class or type of farmer. It is a product which responds to varying kinds and degrees of husbandry, with results corresponding to the amount and character of attention applied to planting and cultivation. It is unlike other crops, as corn for instance, in this respect. A farmer does not have to plan and hustle to grow cotton, though intelligent planning and hustling will produce ever so much more cotton. Many a farmer has worn out his land by repeated crops of cotton without realizing, until too late, that he was actually selling his soil in annual installments. Soil robbery, hillside gullies, individualism, laissez faire, and a colonial economy have gone together in the land of cotton. The land was there to exploit, then why not exploit it, with a climate inviting one to human laziness? The exploitation might apply not only to soil, but to timber, with a Logtown ceasing to have either logs or townsmen.

Clothing and housing requirements are less for those at the bottom level of subsistence than in zones farther north, unless it be emphasized that climate in many parts of the South makes porches a virtual necessity and an institution. (Keenly do I remember with what regret when a boy I had to leave the country front porch and its gossipy conversation on late Sunday afternoons to do the barnyard chores!) However, the much-needed porch is often absent from Southern shacks.

The South does not lead the nation in the purchase and wearing of shoes, as was too pointedly indicated a few years ago by Secretary Frances Perkins, of the Federal Department of Labor. Our articulate majority spokesmen were rather denunciatory of this comment on the lack of shoes, as though barefoot boys in Dixie were unknown in summer time. Well, there are white women and girls working in bare feet in cotton fields and farm houses in sight of the Alabama scene where these words are written. I have seen white men in this community "stepping on the gas" with bare feet in antique Fords. I once heard of a North Georgia farmer who continued to go barefooted after accumulating several thousand dollars. I have seen young men, white and colored, returning from church with shoes tied together and flung over a shoulder to save shoes for future church attendance and to save feet from a pressure to which they were not accustomed. I have heard a scrap of Negro folksong, running as follows:

FORTY ACRES AND STEEL MULES

"O honey, when I had you,
The di'monds you wo';
Now some other scutler's got you,
Barefooted you go."

Public charities, prior to recent trends of urbanization, have been less necessary in the South than elsewhere to prevent actual death from starvation or exposure to the weather. There might be undernourishment, inadequate clothing, and lack of medical attention for scattered thousands, but such cases on the countryside have found a way of remaining in the background. It is a statistical fact that the milk deficiency in the Southern diet is equal to a large part of the national production. Moreover, the South has long had problems of unemployment, which could be classed as serious, though frequently concealed, partial or seasonal. There were periods of idleness on plantations in the days of slavery. However, slaves, like WPA workers of a later day, were sometimes used on beautification and improvement projects, but for private purposes. The labor cost of the plantation project, as of the later works project, could be considered nil in the sense that the laborers under any condition require subsistence.

The unbalanced agriculture of the South has involved not only periods of forced idleness but also rush periods of cultivation or harvesting, with women and children meeting the labor deficit. In fact, excessive ruralism has caused an unusual amount of labor to fall to the lot of women in this region of chivalry. There is a comment handed down from horse and buggy days through aristocratic planter channels to the effect that the men and horses went to town every day, while the women and mules remained at home and worked. The hillbilly counterpart is a story of a man's saying that he did not mind seeing women cook, scrub floors, or draw and carry water, but he could not stand to see them cut wood; in fact, when his wife started such an undertaking he always had to leave the house to keep from witnessing the performance.

The South is diverse in geography, agriculture, and industry. But it is not divided today between planters and hillbillies or between whites

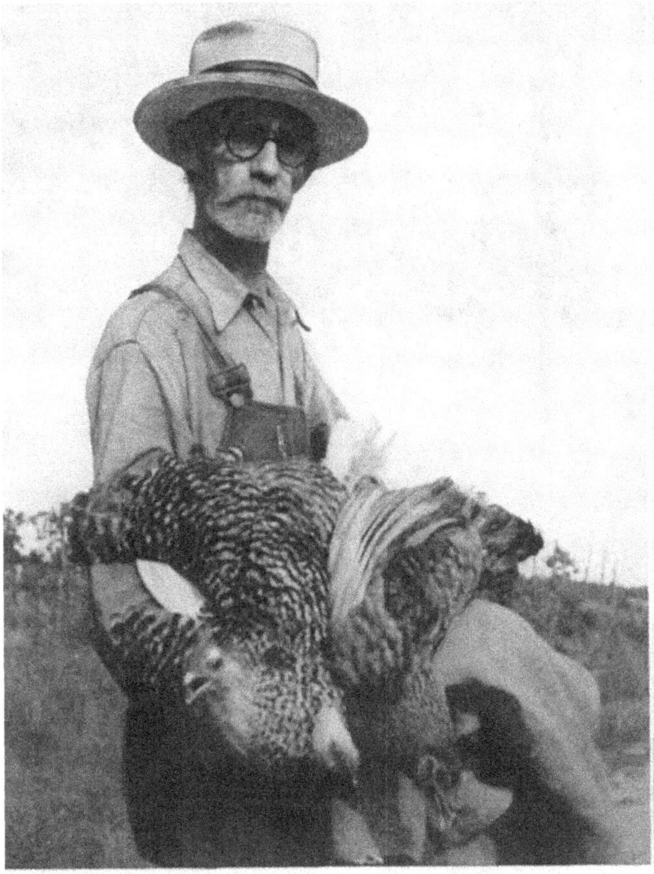

FSA Lange

A man from the hills, now in Greene County, Georgia.

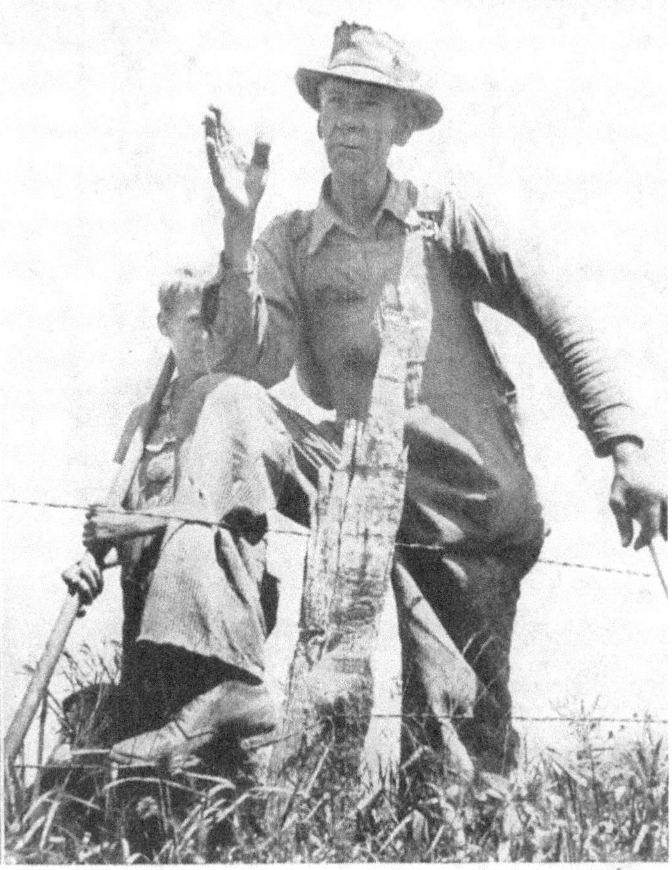

FSA Lange

An Oklahoma farmer tells "what this country needs."

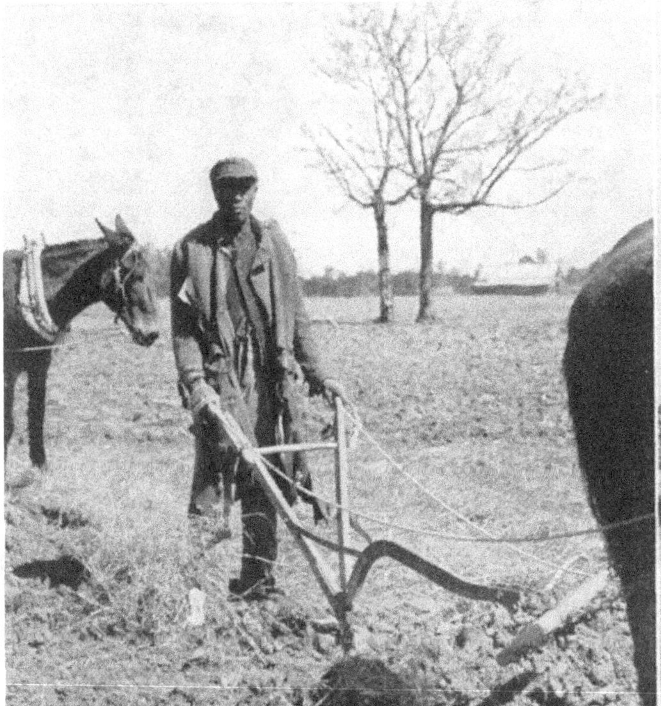

FSA Rothstein

"A forgotten man of the plow handles."

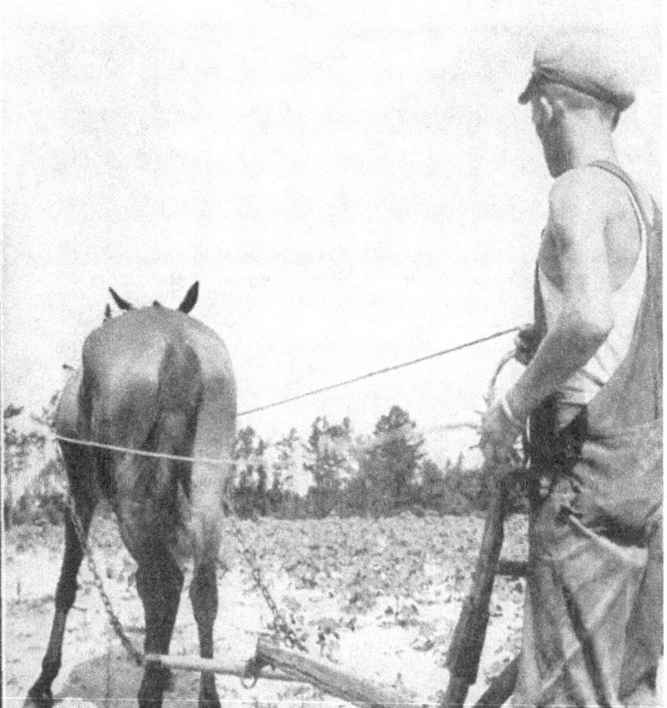

FSA Lange

A white tenant farmer in North Carolina working on shares.

"THE ONE-GALLUS CROPPER OR HILLBILLY FUNCTIONS AS THE LAST SHOCK-ABSORBER."

The gracious charm of white pillars marks a plantation home in Georgia.

Even more important to this landless share cropper in Georgia is the shelter of his ramshackle porch.

Compare the porch of a Negro land owner in the Black Belt with that of the white share cropper on the right.

It is only a step from the porch to the chairs in the shady yard of this Arkansas share cropper.

The dog-run serves as a porch in the cabin of a Georgia tenant farmer.

The sunning of quilts is a common sight in the sun-drenched South.

"CLIMATE IN MANY PARTS OF THE SOUTH MAKES PORCHES A VIRTUAL NECESSITY."

PLAINS, HILLS, AND FARMERS

and Negroes on any basis of sectional segregation. There has been a wide exchange of population between up-country and low-country. Hillbillies are not limited to the highlands. They have moved into the lowlands, to cities, and to other regions, often leaving naked fields abandoned to the healing processes of nature, until misfortune might force them back to refuge in the hills. The up-country in the twentieth century has received an influx of Negroes from the lowlands, many of them becoming hill-country farmers. "Hillbilly" might be enlarged to embrace types of both races, which are pretty well diffused over the hills and valleys and towns of the South.

This civilization, considered in a broad democratic sense, is at the national bottom on all statistical comparisons of wealth, production and culture. It reflects a low per capita income whether measured in cash or in terms of subsistence. It has a comparative shortage of dollars, livestock, poultry and other things. There are many Southern counties in which the gross income per farm inhabitant for such a year as 1929 was less than $100, including the value of farm products consumed in the home. With such low income in the period of prosperity, it is not surprising that during the depression a large proportion of the South's rural population was forced into relief. Farmer independence or self-sufficiency became a myth. The Southern states rank lowest in number of physicians. South Carolina had more than 1,500 inhabitants and Alabama had more than 1,300 per physician in 1936, while the average for the United States was one physician for every 778 inhabitants. Midwives deliver a large proportion of the numerous babies born in the South. Hookworm, malaria, and other preventable ailments, though reduced, are far from negligible. WPA authorities found that practically every family examined for admission to the Arkansas farm colony of Dyess had one or more energy-sapping diseases.

It seems somewhat futile for the Southern champions of "agrarianism" and their opposing advocates of an industrial way of life to argue the issues which divide them, because the South is widely lacking in what either group would wish it to have. The section is so short in subsistence farming and so low in cash farming, that argument for more of one does not cut under the argument for the other. Southerners can no longer ask to be let alone to solve their own problems and then not solve them. The problems offer a challenge and must be faced, locally and nationally. There are the issues of poverty, illiteracy, and race relations, which are closer together than is always assumed. But these hinge on the problems of material productivity, distribution, and well-being, which, in turn, hinge largely on a solution of the ills of farm tenancy in the light of the machine age and on a reduction of that kind of rural commerce which farms the farmer. The subject of farm tenancy will be passed in review in the following chapter, to be followed by a consideration of merchandising and market centers.

CHAPTER THREE

SHARE TENANTS AND CROPPERS

THE SOUTH HAS MORE FARM TENANTS AND POORER TENANTS THAN ANY other section of the country. More than half of the farmers of this region are tenants. The depression and the crop control program of the AAA combined to center national attention on the problem of cotton tenancy, particularly in eastern Arkansas, where a recent rapid expansion of cotton production gave way to a reduction. The problem persists, somewhat as the weather, with nearly every one talking about it and no one finding an immediate and effective way of doing anything about it. It is significant that a majority of the South's farm tenants today are white men. The Negro group switched from a majority to a minority some years ago, though still predominating in the share-cropper bracket of tenancy.* In addition to tenants and croppers, there are more than 200,000 wage-hands on Southern farms and plantations, and whites are numbered in these ranks. White supremacy is rather obsolete as an argument or explanation for the plantation system. There are hillbilly whites in the servile class, and some of them are articulate. These hillbillies, sooner or later, must be served, either by political intelligence or by demagoguery. The Negro minority, moreover, can not be segregated permanently in economic docility.

The acquisitive cotton economy has always had serious shortcomings.

* "Share tenant" is the broader term and is frequently used to include "share cropper."

FORTY ACRES AND STEEL MULES

Before the Civil War one of these shortcomings was slavery, which was supplanted after the war by share tenancy. The break-up of the slavery plantation, as Arthur Raper observes, was a "preface to peasantry," the lowly peasantry of share tenants and croppers. The darker phases of the cotton tenant system have been recently intensified and publicized. The cause of the share cropper has been championed more or less sincerely by left-wing critics of the New Deal and more or less insincerely by commercial Tories whose interest and status have been linked with the expansion of cotton economy and its impoverished tenancy. Members of both of these groups issued volleys of criticism against the AAA for the plight of cotton tenants without seeing the problem as a whole and in historical perspective. It must be remembered that the ills of tenancy are cumulative, compounded of many causes, and accompanied by other ills. The institution of tenancy as it exists in the South has been analyzed and indicted by farm journals and farm prophets for more than a generation. The tenant farmers' unions were preceded many years by up-country Populists and Farmers' Alliance members in calling attention to the forgotten men of the plow-handles. The more recent discussion of tenancy has been characterized by its voluminousness and by the variety of the critics, embracing bankers, college professors, journalists, government officials and labor leaders.* One of the severest words which I have heard on the subject was delivered by the head of a well-managed plantation which is incorporated. The evils of Southern farm tenancy have been extensively explained, but they can not be explained away.

The westward movement of cotton production in the nineteen-twenties left millions of abandoned acres and countless groups of stranded farmers in its wake, with special hardships on many tenants, who generally were poorly prepared to cope with the problems of mechanization, the boll weevil and erosion. The spread of industrial unemployment during the depression reversed the cityward drift of population and pushed thousands of crop-seeking "squatters" into the country. The comparative disadvantage of agriculture since the World War impelled many a landlord

* See the Selected Bibliography at the end of this book for recent writings and documents on farm tenancy.

FSA *Mydans*
A share cropper's shack in Arkansas. "No tools, no equipment, no stock, no garden."

FSA *Rothstein*
This storehouse on a North Carolina farm is probably quite adequate for the farmer's produce and supplies.

FSA *Rothstein*
The barn on a tenant's farm in Walker County, Georgia.

FSA *Rothstein*
A tenant farm in North Carolina. The bell suggests plantation days.

FSA *Rothstein*
This patchwork, or openwork barn on an Alabama tenant farm indicates an unexacting climate.

FSA *Mydans*
A white tenant family of eleven live in this cotton-surrounded house in South Carolina. Gardens interfere with cotton.

"THE PATTERN OF SOUTHERN FARM TENANCY HAS BEEN SET BY SHARE CROPPERS AND SHARE TENANTS..."

FSA *Rothstein*
This "rural slum" near Birmingham at least has sunlight, air, fruit trees, and an outlook on wooded rolling hills.

FSA *Shahn*
The share cropper living in this Arkansas shack "could study astronomy through the roof and geology through the floor."

FSA *Rothstein*
A mountaineer's home in Corbin Hollow, Shenandoah National Park.

FSA *Shahn*
A stove made out of an old oil can. The family could move by "spitting in the fire and calling the dog."

FSA *Lange*
The kitchen of a Georgia plantation house now occupied by an aged Negro couple.

FSA *Shahn*
The porch of a home occupied by a rehabilitation client in Arkansas.

"MANY SOUTHERN TENANTS LIVE OR EXIST IN RURAL SLUMS."

SHARE TENANTS AND CROPPERS

to "take it out" on his tenants, while the impasse of indebtedness in the face of fallen land values and commodity prices precluded large numbers of landlords from administering even the accepted code of landlord-tenant relationships. There are Federal Land Bank authorities who think that in the depression the landlords took a greater "licking" than the tenants, though there is an abundance of Relief Administration evidence to the contrary.

The pattern of Southern farm tenancy has been set primarily by share croppers, secondarily by share tenants, and historically by the Negro dependent group. Those other tenants, who pay a fixed rent in cash or product, are too few in numbers to affect the system, particularly in the Southeast. The share tenant owns or furnishes the equipment and work animals for making the crop, paying a share rent, which is generally one fourth of the cotton and one third of the grain he produces. The share cropper furnishes no equipment or work animals, having everything but labor furnished by the landlord, who receives a rental which is generally one half of the total crop, sometimes more for highly productive lands. The commercial fertilizer bill may be divided between landlord and tenant or cropper on the basis of their respective shares of the crop. The cropper is more dependent upon the landlord for the "furnish" of food and other necessities, which must be paid for out of the cropper's share of the crop. However, a large proportion of share tenants feel a similar dependency. The customary rental is for one year, with no guarantee either to landowner or to tenant of permanency or of remuneration for more than minimum performance. Hence, the minimum performance, on either side, becomes both the rule and the necessity.

Lords of cotton lands have often been able, by circumstance, custom or compulsion, to secure tenant labor for special crops of their own or for other plantation projects at excessively low wages, even for advance credit on time accounts or payment in kind. This relationship is somewhat suggestive of an economy of the "middle ages without the cathedrals." It partly explains the generally low level of farm wages in many parts of the South. The farm tenant system furnished a sort of strategic retreat from Appomattox for Southern planter-colonels and their yeomen colleagues of the up-country. It made possible the perpetuation of economic slavery and the defeat of the major issue of social democracy in Reconstruction. It helped at the same time to hold the cotton kingdom as vassal territory to the larger commercial centers. Cotton tenancy was an important factor in linking the articulate South as a minority partner with the financial East rather than with the agricultural West.

The attempt just after the Civil War to shift the operation of plantations and large farms from slavery to a strict wage-labor basis was short-lived as a general practice. The Federal Commissioner of Agriculture reported in 1867 that in the South the wage system "generally proved unprofitable, the freedmen being inclined to use too freely their newly-found liberty, and planters—quite as little at home in the management of free labor." Moreover, many planters, including important new planters from the North, came to grief with the wage-labor system, coupled with the sudden drop in the price of cotton soon after the war. This speculative bad luck led to a break-up of plantation holdings and an eventual reconcentration on the basis of the tenant method of operation. The only way to carry on a commercial agriculture with plantation units and a minimum of actual cash was on a credit basis, and the crop lien offered the best bid for credit in those times. The share tenant or share cropper became the ultimate shock-absorber, going from year to year with little or no money and with his crop given as security or pledge in advance for his simple purchases. He bore much of the brunt for the local scarcity of liquid capital.

The tenant was more or less at the mercy of his landlord or his local merchant. The landlord's lien on the growing crop, as security for supplies furnished the tenant, was by law made automatically a prior claim without requirement for any written or recorded instrument. The landlord had to "stand" security for his tenants if he wished a merchant other than himself to "furnish" them. The creditor kept the accounts, and it is historically correct to say he preferred or dictated that the debtor or tenant plant a maximum amount of cotton, for such a policy meant more business, even if it also meant unbalanced farming and a lower standard of living for the farmer in the long-run. As Reconstruction yielded to

SHARE TENANTS AND CROPPERS

"white supremacy," Negroes discarded the phrase "forty acres an' a mule" and subscribed to the couplet,

" 'Ought's an 'ought an' figger's a figger;
All fer de white man an' none fer de nigger."

More cotton and one-crop farmers became the order of the day, and it was not infrequently a matter of going to town "to buy some more corn to raise some more cotton to buy some more corn . . ." and so on in an endless cycle of poverty. Garden plots for croppers were sometimes denied or not encouraged, lest gardening interfere with the cultivation of cotton. White tillers became engulfed in the system of tenancy to face low earnings and partial idleness along with Negroes. The system expanded into the hills, capturing the best lands, so to speak, just as had the former system of slavery. Both systems tended to avoid the poorer soil, which thus remained free to support a more diversified farming and a more democratic society.

By 1880 the proportion of tenant farms in the South was forty per cent above the proportion for the country as a whole. Henry W. Grady, noting a "reappearing of the planter princes," observed that the trend of civilization based on cotton culture was still "indeterminate." Writing on "Cotton and Its Kingdom" in *Harper's Magazine* for October, 1881, he raised the question whether cotton "shall bring the South to independence or to beggary," and said further, "Whether its culture shall result in a host of croppers without money or credit, appealing to the granaries of the West against famine, paying toll to usurers at home, and mortgaging their crops to speculators abroad even before it is planted—a planting oligarchy of money-lenders, who have usurped the land through foreclosure, and hold by the ever-growing margin between a grasping lender and an enforced borrower—or a prosperous self-respecting race of small farmers, cultivating their own lands, living upon their own resources, controlling their crops until they are sold, and independent alike of usurers and provision brokers—which of these shall be the outcome of cotton culture the future must determine. . . ."

FORTY ACRES AND STEEL MULES

After half a century, what have we? Not what Henry Grady hoped for, but what he feared. In 1930 Mississippi tenants were seventy-two per cent of all farmers. For Georgia the figure was sixty-eight per cent, for Louisiana sixty-seven per cent, for South Carolina and Alabama sixty-five per cent, for Arkansas sixty-three per cent, and for Oklahoma and Texas sixty-one per cent. The deepening of the depression of the present decade tended to spread the system of tenancy into communities formerly immune from it. Mountain farms became tenant farms to an unheard-of extent, as mountaineers went on relief. Many owners sank into tenancy, while many tenants became farm wage-hands. In nearly all counties of the cotton belt in 1935 more than half the farms were operated by tenants and croppers.

Southern white tenants showed a numerical increase of more than 200,000 in the nineteen-twenties, while Negro tenants registered a slight decrease. The South's million white tenants now outnumber the Negro tenants by more than 300,000. White farmers who own their farms greatly outnumber the Negro owner-operators, and it is now true that white farmers predominate in the production of the South's cotton. A minority of white farmers and a large majority of all Negro farmers, however, are croppers. The average value of Negro cropper farm units, including buildings, in the South in 1935 was only $845, according to agricultural census estimates, though the corresponding average for whites was $1,406. The white croppers of Mississippi cultivated farms of slightly lower average value than the colored croppers.

Share croppers and share tenants on encumbered holdings fare ill in hard times, and they have a rather high mobility in good times. Much of this mobility is restricted to the local community or county. There are efficiently operated tenant plantations, with landlords or supervisors on the ground, and there are examples of successful share tenants and croppers with little or no supervision. I know tenants, a few Negro tenants, who own their own stock and equipment free of debt and have made a living for years on lands of absentee owners. But, for the South as a whole, such cases are exceptional. Absentee ownership and gross inefficiency are associated on too many middle-size holdings of the region, holdings which

On a tenant farm in North Carolina.

Carrying drinking water at Gee's Bend, Alabama.

Water from a spring, Shenandoah National Park.

In the Ozarks. The old oaken bucket has gone modern, but the iron kettle for washday has not.

An Arkansas share cropper with his homemade water wagon. If the mule won't pull it, perhaps the goats will.

A rural water supply in Georgia.

Sanitation is notable for its absence.

Note the well at the left of the cabin.

"IT IS OCCASIONALLY NECESSARY FOR TENANTS TO GO HUNDREDS OF YARDS FOR GOOD DRINKING WATER."

Sugar cane worker's cabin, Louisiana.

In the Louisiana sugar cane country.

Well-kept home owned by a Negro, Beaufort, South Carolina.

A typical North Carolina farmhouse, showing excellent adaptation to the climate.

A dog-run house in Alabama, in which a Negro tenant farmer lives.

A share cropper's shack in Arkansas.

An old plantation house in Georgia. Two rooms are occupied by an aged Negro couple.

Home of a Negro farmer on St. Helena Island, off Beaufort, South Carolina.

IN THE SOUTH HOUSING REQUIREMENTS ARE LESS AT THE BOTTOM LEVEL OF SUBSISTENCE THAN IN THE NORTH

SHARE TENANTS AND CROPPERS

can not carry the overhead of expert management, and yet can not be operated effectively without management. Too much plantation supervision is not scientific but amateurish and intermittent.

Many Southern tenants live or exist in rural slums, often adjacent to standing timber and other building resources. Large families often make out with two or three rooms. It has been said without serious damage to truth that many a tenant could study astronomy through the openings in the roof and geology through holes in the floor of his tumble-down shack, while the scarcity of furniture would permit a removal by the simple process of spitting in the fire and calling the dog. One can see, however, a few tenant houses, which have screened doors and windows. There are instances of tenants living in respectable homes, which were formerly occupied by the owners. These houses generally have only fading evidences of paint. Sanitary privies are frequently lacking, and it is occasionally necessary to go hundreds of yards for good drinking water. The diet is at times restricted to "meat, meal and molasses," the meat being "sowbelly." There may be field peas, and there may be rabbits and opossums in season, for many a cropper has a hound or two. Milk to drink may be as scarce as champagne, with sweet potatoes as the nearest possible substitute for milk for small children. Lack of education is sometimes the explanation for the unbalanced diet of tenant families. The majority of these families of the South have a very low plane of living, as measured by their houses, their food, their clothing, and the things they do without.

If a cropper's gross cotton earnings, including the landlord's share, amount to only $153.60, the average for a Mississippi county in 1933, any kind of a standard of living is impossible. Decent living would be difficult on the basis of cotton earnings for five other sample counties in Southern states, with the county average ranging from $166.50 to $822.50 per tenant before deducting the rent, as brought out by field studies. There is little room for optimism in a WPA study released in 1937, showing that the average income of wage-hands, share croppers and other tenants in eleven Southern areas in 1934 was $309 per family or $73 per person. This average seems low, but many farmers fall below it. Farm tenancy in the South is "an expression of poverty." With more machinery, more white farmers, and a higher production per man, the Southwest has tenant problems somewhat different from those of the Southeast, but none the less critical, particularly among farmers who lack the capital and the equipment, for modernized farming is not immune from failure.

The farm tenant system of the South affects the attitude and outlook of landlords somewhat as slavery influenced the minds of masters. The servile class is held to have the predestined lot for which it seems fitted and from which there can and should be no rise or escape. Landlords of long experience can be heard to say that the inferior status of share croppers, white as well as black, is inevitably due to an inferior ability. This view precludes any public interest in an "agricultural ladder" for the unfortunates. Indifference, if not opposition, to reform is natural. Exploitation, perchance softened by paternalism, seems to be the landlord's right and the tenant's expectation. Many landlords have opposed upsetting the landlord-tenant relationship, as Emergency Relief Administration investigators discovered. Landlords generally do not wish this relationship disturbed, and many tenants have developed a psychological attitude of dependence.

The typical landlord's idea of tenancy is only a half-truth. It is more accurate to say that tenancy breeds ignorance and ignorance breeds more tenancy, that both keep farmers submerged, and that neither tenancy nor ignorance can be cured without curing the other. Lack of education and lack of economic hope combine to kill initiative and to prevent interest in livestock, machinery, farm improvements, or farm organization. Tenants, if they would, could not easily act together for group production, buying, processing, or selling, except to the limited extent a landlord may enforce common action among his own croppers, as in sharing and exchanging work, largely for economy in the use of the landlord's tools and equipment.

Once a share cropper, always a share cropper, is almost an apt analysis, if allowance be made for shifts to common wage labor in industry or agriculture. Harold Hoffsommer, in an Alabama Relief Administration study of several hundred cases, found that "of those who started farming as share

SHARE TENANTS AND CROPPERS

croppers, nearly three fourths still remain such." Less than one tenth had become owners. He correctly condemns the system as disadvantageous to both landlord and tenant. The former has to depend on an unstable and irresponsible type of tenant, and any landlord who individually endeavors to raise the level or status of his tenants may suffer loss. There are enlightened planters who have tried uplift policies only to have their improved tenants enticed away by other planters. The unscrupulous landlord has tended to profit more than the socially minded landlord and to set the pace, while it has been the most incompetent cropper who has tended to set the pace, or to slow the pace, for tenants in the vicious system.

The tenants are largely victims of a social rather than a biological heritage. Their shiftlessness is primarily the result of generations of tenancy, of a reconciled sense of exploitation, of going to bed tired and getting up without hope. The individual landlord is unable to check the influence of the system, by which personality traits of tenancy and dependency, so to speak, are acquired, developed, and handed down, with an increasing accommodation to a dependent status as a normal condition. Individual and social inertia results. Yet the basis of dependency is distinctly precarious, as was brought home to thousands of tenants after 1929.

It is false to assume that share croppers and share tenants are humanly hopeless. Croppers, of both races, have become managing share tenants under my observation, and share tenants have become owners and operators of farms. Large family groups in the up-country often include thrifty owners of poor lands and typical tenants of good lands, the human difference being entirely of environmental cause. Children of tenant families have moved out of the stratum under the stimulus of education. I can point out share croppers whose lack of education, not of native ability, is the chief reason for their remaining share croppers. Though thousands are inevitably doomed, other thousands are capable of elevation through improvement in their opportunity and environment. Malaria and the hookworm have put the poorer rural people of the South at a decided disadvantage, and other ailments, such as pellagra, represent the effect of poor folks' restricted food habits. These and other environmental factors may explain much of that backwardness which has been attributed to heredity. There is no special evidence of inherent inferiority of the "poor whites" of the South as a class, if allowance be made for economic and social conditions. There is no rigid racial subdivision between "poor whites" and other whites who are poor, though there may be results of differences in the intensity and period of exposure to poverty. A certain amount of social sifting has taken place over the years with the large migration from the countryside. The exodus has included many of the active, skilled and best educated members of tenant families, though many willing farmers remain on the land. I recall members who have become urban carpenters, grocery salesmen, peace-time soldiers, textile workers and followers of "public works." They have found improvement of status away from the farm, not on it. Many who know little but stereotyped methods of farming are left behind for landlords to choose from, and the unchosen include not a few incompetents, who emphasize the degradation of the picture.

It is not safe to generalize too freely about farm tenancy in the South in view of the economic and geographical variety of the institution. But there is little argument for retaining it in its prevailing form. There is no constructive feature of it which can not be as well or better provided by other methods. It signifies no efficient or large-scale production but only a conglomeration of small farming units, a centralized control, in part, of the business phases and of the profits, if and when there are any. It discourages the use of intensive types and methods of agriculture, which are imperative for successful small-scale farming. It offers the tenant few or no incentives to conserve or improve the land, buildings, or other property of the owner, and it offers the owner little gain or profit for making the physical life more comfortable for his tenants. "The tenant skins the land, and the landlord skins the tenant," it has been said, and he who can skins the landlord. It is the dynamics of poverty. But it has filled a large place in our Southern economy and it can not be wished away.

Elevation of the share cropper class can not be achieved in a day. Many

SHARE TENANTS AND CROPPERS

issues are involved in the South's systemic disease of tenancy and in any reduction or redirection of it. Tenancy and our whole farm life are intimately linked with rural commerce, towns and villages. It is important to observe the role which these factors play and fail to play in the farm drama of the South.

CHAPTER FOUR

MERCHANTS AND MARKETS

THE SOUTH'S ONE-CROP EMPHASIS GIVES THIS REGION A COMMERCIAL agriculture and in consequence an agricultural commerce. A majority of its towns and villages owe origin and growth to market demands for farm products, farmer purchases, and the financing of these economic activities. Such is the background of old New Orleans, largest city of the cotton country; of Memphis, Montgomery, Charleston and Mobile; of Natchez with its historic grandeur; of a Selma, Alabama, or a Rome, Georgia; of a newer Farmersville here and there. Most of the South's industrial centers receive no small degree of economic support directly and indirectly from agriculture.

The Southern farm market centers are entrepôts and exchange stations of an acquisitive system into which move the products of the labor of wage-hands and croppers, of tenants and "independent" farmers. This system of business enterprise is conspicuous in the South, though not peculiar to this section. It is an economy by which the actual farmer is so placed that, as producer and consumer, he is confronted with business concerns and business forces which fix the terms of the traffic going and coming. Such a practice of exchange means, particularly in the cotton South, that it becomes the practice of the country town to make the most of the necessity, disadvantage, and ignorance of the surrounding farm population. There is a strong tendency for the commercial townsmen to count on an inordinately wide margin of gain over outlay and over the value of the services rendered the farm population. Southern economy reveals another side to this kind of agricultural commerce. The country town, it must be noted, is unable to retain its commercial gains but passes a good part of them to massive interests in other centers and other regions. These interests, which "move obscurely in the background of the market," exploit the country town in a manner analogous to that in which the country town exploits the farm population. The whole process doubly emphasizes the unfortunate quantity ratio of commodity exchange against the farmer, compelling him to bring to market a disproportionately large amount of cotton or other products to pay for shoes, overalls, farm machinery, or perchance an automobile. "Dirt" farmers, though not students or masters of institutional economics, naïvely sense the workings of this business process. They express their ideas on the subject in various ways. Said a cotton farmer of Possum Trot, when his credit merchant drove by in a new Buick, "I paid for one fourth of that car." *

The policy of farming the farmer has not only severely affected Negro and white tenants, but its burden has also been keenly felt by landowning farmers, particularly through usurious store credit. The production of cotton in the era of slavery was often based on the use of credit, and the subsequent expansion of production has been accompanied by an increasing dependence on credit facilities. Production credit during slavery was essentially aristocratic, the landowning master being the ultimate borrower. But the termination of slavery and the break-up or modification of the plantation system brought a democratization of crop loan methods, with the "one-gallus" cropper or hillbilly functioning as the last shock-absorber.

The new South, from Appomattox to the World War and after, has relied more heavily than did the old South on an agriculture which counted cotton as the chief "legal tender," with tobacco an important cash crop in certain sub-regions. Cotton acreage and production were more than trebled during this period, and in 1933 the new South plowed

* This sense of exploitation is available for rural demagogues, especially in hard times. They do not have to create it. It is already there. They use it.

up about as much cotton as the old South ever had. To its trade in this staple the new South added a cotton seed business, which developed with the rise of the cotton oil industry and has reached a commercial magnitude equal to that which could be claimed for cotton in the eighteen-fifties. It has been said that cotton seed was garbage in 1860, fertilizer in 1870, cattle feed in 1880, table food in 1890. Because of a less standardized market, there has often been a wider spread between the price paid the farmer and the price received by the buyer for seed than in the case of cotton. The seed sales have been somewhat freer than cotton from the channels of mortgages and liens and have not infrequently been the only source of actual cash received by debtor farmers in autumn.

The agricultural South has always had a shortage of cash and working capital. This shortage was especially marked just after the Civil War, and created a demand for outside credit. Leading Southerners went to the happy hunting grounds of New York and elsewhere for financial aid, expanding a practice maintained by planters on a smaller scale before 1860. Northern and even foreign factors financed the furnishing of supplies to tenant farmers and other farmers, whose crops were security for the debts. Large factors sprang up in Southern cities, especially New Orleans and Memphis, while similar functionaries operated on a smaller scale in large inland towns. The scarcity of country banks in the South prior to 1900 gave the factors their opportunity. Besides serving as bankers for their clients, they also handled the cotton produced and even at times exercised control over purchases of supplies and of transportation. They were participants in a profit system which seemed immediately to depend on the volume of business. They were more interested in a maximum cotton delivery by their clientele than in livestock and diversified crops for actual farmers. They knew that home production and consumption of foods and feeds do not directly swell the stream of commerce. They insisted by contract on big cotton quotas with penalties for quota deficits, regardless of payment for the general indebtedness. Their dictates were relayed by their clients, who had to exact all the toll the traffic would bear. Many planters, tenants and other farmers were in debt together. Henry W. Grady, just before his death, observed that Southern merchants

Home of a Georgia cotton farmer who has raised cotton on his own farm for fifty years.

A share crop farm near Gaffney, South Carolina, which is too rough and irregular for a steel mule.

The plantation owner's daughter checks the weight of cotton which she has picked, Kaufman County, Texas.

Checking in the cotton, Little Rock, Arkansas.

Cotton at the gin, Robstown, Texas.

Greenville, Mississippi, an important cotton shipping center.

"Here comes the show boat!"

Circuses make the rounds of Southern farm towns in the autumn to attract the farmers and their cash.

A blind street musician, West Memphis, Arkansas.

A medicine show in Huntington, Tennessee.

This sign on a Louisiana butcher shop compares favorably with the cave paintings of Altamira.

A small-town amusement denied to isolated farm tenants and share croppers.

"COTTON BREEDS MONOTONY, AND TENANT FARMERS SOMETIMES GO TO TOWN..."

were prosperous, while the farmers were poor. As the *Report of the Commissioner of Agriculture* of the United States for 1886 said of the cotton country, the soil was "wearing away, with the lives of the cultivators, for the benefit of the commercial class." Even the wearing away of soil seemed to increase commerce, for the $300,000,000 cotton crop of 1880 was accompanied by a fertilizer cost of $32,000,000, giving the South the primacy in fertilizer business. The production of cotton has continued to call for a large bill for commercial fertilizer. The South today uses more than half the commercial fertilizer of the nation, and the cost for this item approximates one tenth of the returns from cotton in Southeastern communities and states. A Negro farmer, whom I once asked why he was buying so much fertilizer, said, "I have to buy it to raise cotton to pay debts with."

The key men of this acquisitive system in the farm community centers have been the town and country merchants, many of whom have also been landlords. The operation of cotton ginning has often been associated with a combination of landholding and merchandising, with the business thus extended to trading in cotton seed. The key man might thus be virtually the whole economic world to his tenant-customers. "Merchant and planter" became a rather common expression in the cotton belt after 1865 to denote a rural baron, or a Main Street man of influence and power. Such a leader's store and office might be considered as a little commercial capital, and, if there was ever an "economic man" in the flesh, he must have been a supply merchant in the cotton country with a crop lien to give him a business monopoly. The typical method for the "come-back" of old families as well as for the "arrival" of new ones after the Civil War was through a combination of farm holdings and rural merchandising. A new up-country commercial gentry has tended to hold its own with lowlanders in ability to be hard-boiled.

The South's colonial economy has made the "merchant and planter" the equivalent of a concessionaire in a backward country. He has had more risk than competition in dealing with dependent clients. If his business failed, it was because of speculation of some kind or inefficient management in the face of fluctuations in weather, crops, and prices.

FORTY ACRES AND STEEL MULES

"Time prices" charged by merchants to farmers have been known to run as high as twenty-five and even fifty per cent above retail cash prices, though the period over which credit was granted was generally less than a year, often only a few months.

The case history of a landholding supply merchant who was active in the last quarter of the nineteenth century is revealing. His store was in a town of about a thousand population. There was no bank in the town. The merchant carried an account with a New York bank, often selling checks to smaller fellow merchants and cashing checks for good exchange rates. His merchandise tended to reflect higher cash prices than did items in other stores, for he specialized in credit accounts and avoided too much emphasis on the high "mark-up" for sales "on time." He had tenants and other farmers for customers. He bought their cotton in the fall and disposed of it through New York and built up his bank account in that city. He was also a money lender and took mortgages on many crops and farms, not infrequently foreclosing on them. He became a man of wealth, though many of his clients went "broke." A local Negro preacher was once reported as offering thanks in prayer for the existence of a good country that was ever free from the evils of mortgages and liens, in the presence of this same supply merchant, who was named in the prayer of thanks.

This was not an isolated case for the period, though many were less successful and less important. However, toward the end of the century, merchant credit to farmers came into competition with loan company credit, and country banks were springing up to extend aid to farmers. But actually high interest rates continued to prevail for years, frequently disguised on the face of the mortgage note for legal or other reasons. I can cite an up-country merchant and farmer who expanded both branches of his business at a new railway junction by borrowing money from a "banking and loan" agency at an interest rate of seventeen per cent. And this money was turned into a profit through the operation of a country store. The failure of a neighboring rural entrepreneur can be explained by citing an overextension of land holdings on a credit basis and an easy-going management. The case of the loss of a fortune by a merchant and planter through dealings in cotton "futures" on "margins" was not an isolated example.

The dominant members of this merchant and planter class have tended to look to the financial East rather than to the agricultural West for economic politics. They generally opposed the farmers' crusade which came to the front in the Farmers' Alliance and the Populist party organizations, and those organizations of hillbillies were partly directed against large merchants and planters, as were the subsequent Farmers' Union and the more recent Southern Farm Tenants' Union. The conservative opponents of the agrarian crusade of the Populists used Negro votes to check both the economic and the political effects of the movement, just as industrialists at the same time were using Negro workers to break strikes in Southern industry and depress the wages for whites.

The merchant's immediate control of the farmer's economic life was somewhat reduced or modified after 1900 by the improvement of bank facilities for rural credit, the coming of industry to the South, and the spread of education for Negroes. By different ways, many farmers were finding it possible to pay cash for merchandise or to exercise choice as to where they might trade on time. Industrial developments, especially in the up-country, gave farm families opportunity to sell various products and to find part-time employment for ready cash so as to minimize dependence on the credit of supply merchants. There are instances of farmers near growing urban centers increasing income by giving up the cultivation of cotton and catering to city needs for fruit, vegetables and milk. The chain-store invasion of agricultural villages was further evidence of a limitation of the old-line merchant and planter monopoly, though chain stores are less prevalent in Southern farm villages than in villages of other regions.

The advantages of these changes in commerce for farmers have been mainly restricted to owners and upper-class tenants. Most croppers, many tenants, and even small landowning farmers have been unable to avail themselves of the modern methods. Share croppers have not generally been eligible even for government seed loans in their own names. If the depression wrecked the store credit these groups had been used to, there was nothing left for them but government relief or rural rehabilitation. The psychological implications of the landlord-tenant relationship, with assumptions of paternalism and dependency, have similarly permeated the supply merchant-customer relationship. Negro croppers have especially tended to take for granted a status of dependency, both for land and for merchandise or basic cash needs, without much bickering as to the amount of interest rate or merchandise mark-up. About three years ago a hard-working Negro share cropper of my acquaintance had to have money to pay a lawyer to get him out of a criminal mess for which he was not at all to blame. He paid to his furnishing landlord $50 for a loan of $37.50 for a year. Both lender and borrower seemed to consider the loan a favor. A rural Negro, according to a story, once praised a white man highly and sincerely, saying, "He loaned me ten dollars two years ago, and he ain't never asked me for it;—'course I keeps the interest paid up—fifty cents a month." The spread of tenancy and the social attitudes of tenancy made it impossible for cash business to supplant the merchandise credit business.

The rural South has continued to utilize general merchandise stores of the village and the countryside. This custom is reflected, for instance, in the census statistics of 1930. Analyzing these figures, Brunner and Kolb, in their *Rural Social Trends*, say, "the South, which shows the lowest value of retail sales per capita in every other category, indicates its continuing dependence on general country stores for its supplies by maintaining higher per capita retail sales in this traditional category than any other region." Many of these country stores are cotton plantation stores and survive because the tenant-customers can trade nowhere else. Few of them are coöperative enterprises. In the coöperative purchase of farm supplies the cotton states fall considerably below the grain and livestock states in both the value and the percentage of the purchases. A bulletin based on the census of 1930 shows Mississippi coöperative purchases to be less than one tenth of the Iowa purchases.

The connection between the plantation store and plantation tenancy or wage-labor can not easily be overemphasized. It is sometimes overlooked. That plantation merchandising is a convenient adjunct of this

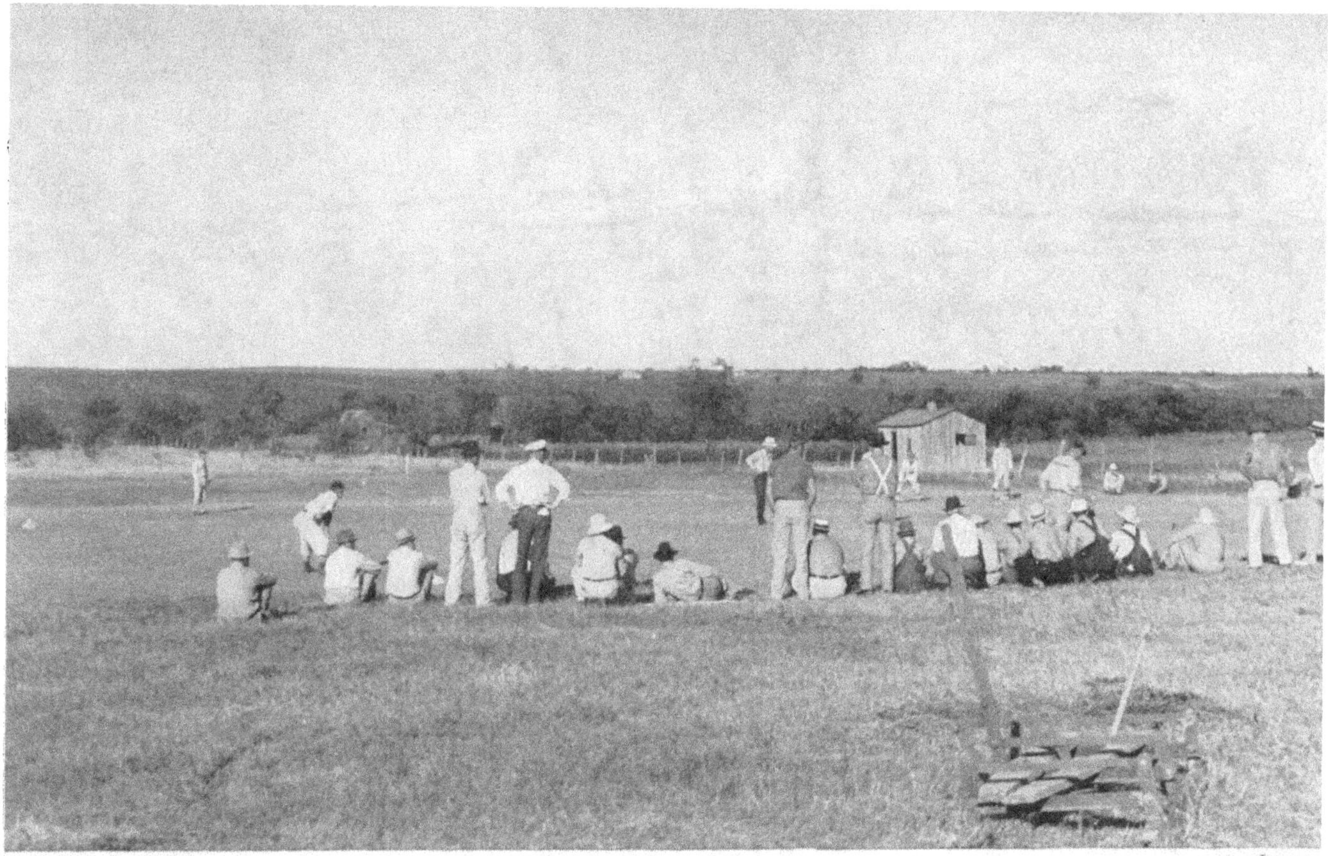

FSA Lange

This Sunday afternoon baseball game in Texas is a typical form of recreation wherever there is a community of sufficient density to furnish a team.

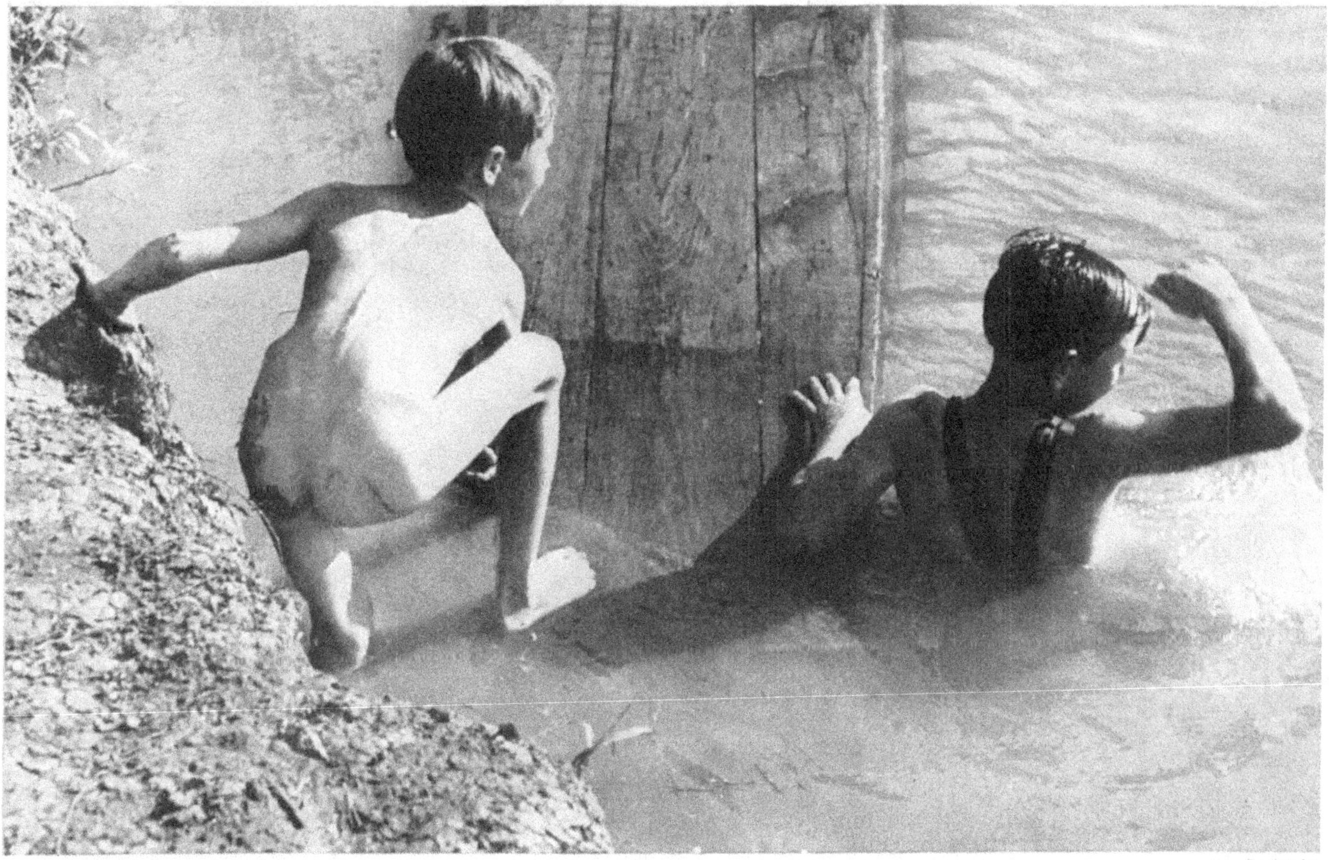

FSA Rothstein

One of the inalienable rights of boyhood, a swimming hole, is provided at the Dyess Colony in Arkansas.

A house in the village of Nethers, Shenandoah National Park. "We ain't exactly scrouged."

Abundant leisure, just "settin' around," in front of the Nethers post office.

Winslow, Arkansas. Most of the South's towns and villages owe origin and growth to farm market demands.

Loafers' Wall, Batesville, Arkansas. The long summer rather than the hot summer moderates the tempo of human activity.

"Fortunes have been made—and lost—in plantation stores."

"The South has continued to utilize general merchandise stores."

SEVENTY PER CENT OF THE SOUTHERN POPULATION LIVES IN THE COUNTRY OR IN SMALL VILLAGES.

MERCHANTS AND MARKETS

system of farming is evinced by the fact that the Resettlement Administration has seen proper to use the practice in a few cases. Southern farm workers would have exceedingly great difficulty and would lose much time from work if they had to go great distances for smoking tobacco, chewing tobacco and snuff. It facilitates the work in busy seasons for these and other necessities to be had on or near the plantation, either from a regular store or from a more informal commissary. The mercantile establishment may also serve as a convenient agency by which the planter procures items of equipment, tools, plows, harness, seed and the like, which are continuously needed for the farm operations. For a cotton plantation of any size a store is an economy.

It is true that tenants and croppers frequently pay in about as much on store accounts in the fall as they pay on share rent. It is also true that debtors to plantation stores in many cases never know what they owe or what they really pay. "Black-smith" methods of bookkeeping are not infrequently used by country merchants, who, because of a multiplicity of duties, are often behind with their bookkeeping. They can not easily let their customers know how the accounts stand, even if there be no wish to conceal. In the absence of competition or regulation, why should an expensive system of accounting be maintained? There are, of course, many merchants who have modernized their methods, who select their customers and tenants with care, and who hold the credit rate down to something like a flat ten per cent. But there are instances of continued backwardness and high time prices, even by merchant-planters who get government agricultural credit at low rates of interest. Part of the confusion and criticism in connection with the government benefit payments to share tenants and croppers for crop reduction in the South resulted from the role of the credit merchant and his methods of collection on accounts.

Fortunes have been made through the operation of plantation stores, no less than through the farming operations, and fortunes have also thus been lost. The low productivity of the average farm family, boll weevil invasions, and the wide fluctuations of cotton prices in recent years have made plantation merchandise business rather speculative and precarious.

FORTY ACRES AND STEEL MULES

Plantation merchants have justified their usurious time prices on the grounds of serious risk and frequent losses. If thriftless tenants of absentee landlords have contributed to this justification, it has been hard on the other tenants to face a credit cost of twenty-five or fifty per cent to even up gains and losses for the merchant. The slipshod system allows the lazy and unscrupulous to beat the game and it penalizes the worthy tenants, working unfortunate influences on both groups. The unscrupulous merchant, as in the case of the unscrupulous planter or tenant, tends to set the standards of the game.

The one-crop economy causes farmers to be "broke" most of the year, for there is a shortage of cash except at harvest time. The up-and-down status of community cash and bank deposits between autumn and other seasons frequently leads farm families to practice a severe self-denial of necessities during nine months of the year and to resort to rather free and unwise expenditures when cotton is sold, if finances permit. The dissipation of the autumn surplus puts the farmer right back into a debtor status for the next crop. I have known tenant farmers, white share tenants, to go to town and "drink up" their autumn surplus of fifty and even a hundred dollars in one grand spree. A hillbilly group once celebrated their crop year by visiting the nearest little city and reserving for the night a "red-light" house with all its feminine personnel, returning next day to their hard-working women folk in the country. The gadgets of amusement occasionally bought by cotton tenants are striking evidence of a temporary flush-time carelessness. Circuses make the rounds of Southern farm towns in the autumn to attract the farmers and their cash, at the same time furnishing a break which is richly deserved.

The plantation-store method of carrying on commerce tends to emphasize the one-crop system, and the one-crop emphasis favors such a commercial policy. The two features together constitute an economic system which can stand neither prosperity nor panic nor depression. The commerce and the soil are likely to be abused through expansion in good times, with a consequent breakdown of the economic process in hard times. The profit-and-loss policy of time furnishing tends to force farmers to mine the soil for money crops rather than to conserve the soil by scien-

MERCHANTS AND MARKETS

tific farming. It is a coördinate factor, along with tenancy, in effecting an erosion of the hills as well as an erosion of the minds and spirits of hillbillies. It is a practice which limits the productivity of the goose which is supposed to lay the golden egg. In the end, it limits the real income of both the farmer and the merchant.

Southern agriculture emphasizes commerce, but the South ranks below the rest of the country in rural retail trade per capita. Village commerce was hit early and hard by the depression in one-crop areas, particularly in the cotton country. Brunner and Kolb noted that "in two villages in one cotton state, eight general stores, three groceries, two drug stores and agencies of both Ford and General Motors had undergone bankruptcy between 1925 and 1929," and that another Southern town of about 1,000 population had fifteen bankruptcies since 1924. They found village bank failures heaviest in the Middle West and the South.

The farming and the farm commerce of the South vitally affect the town and village life of the region. The unbalanced system of trade and agriculture points to a village system which lacks a well-rounded activity. It is in order to attempt an appraisal of the Southern community life which is based largely on one-crop farming and one-crop commerce.

CHAPTER FIVE

TOWNS AND VILLAGES

"You seem to have plenty of room up here," remarked a traveller who stopped at a North Alabama farm home for a road inquiry after having covered four or five miles without seeing a house. The woman of the house replied, "We ain't exactly scrouged."

The South is a region of open spaces and scattered homesteads. Seventy per cent of the population lives in the country or in urban centers of less than 2,500 inhabitants. The one-crop agriculture, offering limited support to an all-year commerce, does not stimulate an extensive and vigorous town or village activity. This region, in comparison with many others of the nation, has a paucity of farm villages to match a relatively small retail trade among rural customers. This condition partly explains the low railway traffic density in many portions of the agricultural South and certain freight differentials against this section. In combination with the freight discrimination, it partly explains the failure of the South to pay as high wages on all counts as the rest of the country. It is connected with the comparatively small per capita income below the Potomac.

Writings of travellers of the nineteenth century are replete with comments on the distances between the South's small towns. Frederick Law Olmsted, in his journeys through the cotton country prior to 1860, found stretches of wilderness to confirm his Yankee prejudices. The general rural isolation was a contributing factor to the traditional Southern hospitality, strangers and visitors being a welcome break in the monotony,

TOWNS AND VILLAGES

perhaps, of partial idleness. The first capital of the Confederacy was a town and farm market center of only eight thousand inhabitants when Jefferson Davis was inaugurated as president in 1861. As late as 1880 the lower South's population of eight million embraced a total of only half a million in cities of eight thousand inhabitants or more. This region early became one of farmers and plantations, but it has not yet lost complete kinship with the frontier. In large portions of the South the county, not the town, furnishes the predominant unit of government and the most descriptive label for designating prominent citizens in state-wide news. Obituary items frequently contain such phrases as "prominent Madison countian" or "leading planter of Dallas County." To explain the boyhood background of Associate Justice Black it is important to mention Clay County, Alabama, which connotes a prevalent white population, minimum of urbanization, and maximum dependence upon hill farmers.

Southern villages, long steeped in individualism, have sponsored a minimum amount of coöperative business enterprise among and for farmers. Tenants in the South do not and can not easily take an interest in coöperative activities and societies which have remade many rural communities. The community services of the different state universities, land grant colleges, and experiment stations make little headway in tenant communities. The wonderful farm demonstration work of Seaman A. Knapp some years ago was circumscribed by the existence of tenancy. Not only the tenants, but also their landlords are likely to stand in the way of coöperative organizations and activities among independent small farmers. The typical landlord's business policy and village coöperatives are somewhat antagonistic. The existence of two races of farmers is a further check to mutual organization. It is pathetic, for instance, to observe the unorganized backwardness of Negro tenants and Negro hamlets virtually under the shadow of Tuskegee Institute in Macon County, Alabama. It is difficult for the light of Tuskegee to penetrate share cropper darkness.

Southern farm villages and little towns are frequently the most dreary eyesores in sections where the one-crop system predominates. Filling or service stations sometimes constitute the redeeming feature, in appearance, though they may also be specimens of ugliness. The mercantile establishments need not make a bid of attractiveness to farmer credit customers, who may have no choice as to which store to patronize. Individual and social overheads are reduced to a minimum, seldom including comfort stations for Negro women, who are likely to supply a good portion of the Saturday afternoon population. A cotton gin brings autumn bustle and hustle, but lacks the signs of life at other seasons. Very likely, too many church steeples point the way heavenward for the few steady worshippers, and the clergymen are often too slow to champion the cause of the underprivileged except for the other world. A dogmatic clergy and an intense rural religiosity have contributed much to illiberalism in Southern communities. The virtual divorce of religion from social morality has not been limited to Negro churches. The clergy of both races in the rural South have too often steered clear of applied religion. Many a rural white has read and reread the Bible while living an anti-social life. There have been rural preachments on social issues, however, and Arkansas planters are known to have enjoined certain ministers with tenant audiences to stick to the gospel and stay off economic subjects.

The market village, if its history antedates the Civil War, very likely has one or a few old white mansions, with spacious porches and high columns. It must also have a few citizens who know how to be gracious in elegant society and perhaps likewise how to live on the labor of others. If it is a new center in a district developed since slavery, the entrepreneurs may be economic go-getters, little saturated with the spirit of human welfare or of noblesse oblige. The country shopper is likely to fare better in the new town of better business than in the sleepy one of better families. In either case the merchants and landlords constitute the most articulate life of the town, and these groups are generally rather reluctant to loosen up voluntarily with handsome donations for public purposes and the common good. They are neither overwilling taxpayers nor ardent champions of social progress. Their profit motive, as a rule, is poorly satisfied in the net sense, and they feel little obligation to better the civic life of customers and tenants. It is hard for a merchant-planter

TOWNS AND VILLAGES

to appreciate the recreational needs of dependent families. The owner of a thousand acres sometimes denies tenant boys an acre in an old field or pasture for Saturday afternoon baseball.

Farm tenants, particularly the share tenants and croppers of the Southeast, have little civic power and take little interest in public matters. Negro tenants, as a rule, are denied the suffrage, and many whites fail to qualify for voting, to participate in any organization, or even to subscribe to a newspaper or periodical, unless it be a sheet that is had for twenty-five cents a year. They have few facilities for recreation on the plantation, which, in a sense, is the tenants' village. Little provision is made for their leisure, and they seem to know only idleness when not at work. Negro tenants seem to find happier ways of passing the time away than the whites. I once interviewed a group of white tenants, all relatively prosperous, on the subject of their leisure time. They mentioned hunting, rambling, "settin' around" and "piddling," little else. Less than a third were voters or church members.

The most available conversational center for the men and boys of cropper families is frequently the big barn of the plantation. It is headquarters for the goings and comings with the landlord's mules. The workers may meet here for a noon hour or more in the crop-working season and on occasions when rain forces them in from work before quitting time. The barn thus becomes a sort of club, sometimes a harmonious interracial club, for gossip about the weather, crops, personalities, and mules, which may be referred to by proper names or as "jar-heads" or "hard-tails." The wit or humor of the barnyard consists of a mixture of the stale and the racy, some of it not quite printable. There are no club lockers, but sometimes there are convenient nooks where bottles of liquor may be concealed.

"Holy-roller" religious meetings catch the attention of not a few white croppers, tenants and others. Summer revivals and all-day singings, "with dinner on the ground" make strong appeal to hillbillies, farm villagers and hick-town men. The cooking arts and the menus vary slightly in the different backwoods communities. A sophisticated visiting divine once decided that the ardent professions of religion were too great to harmonize genuinely with the eating of soggy biscuits, which were supplied so freely. He suspended soul salvation temporarily to inaugurate instructions on preparing bread that would be more suitable to the stomach. Hillbilly singing affairs are often characterized by vim, vigor, speed and perspiration. Many of the tunes suggest jazz music for dancing. The singing and the social life of a country revival generally surpass the sermons in human interest as much as the sport section and the comic pages surpass in appeal the editorials of a Sunday newspaper. Young men have been known to fake repentance and visit the "mourners' bench" in order to encourage the ministers in charge of the revival to prolong the socially interesting series, which was about to close for lack of spiritual interest. I know of one instance in which the trick worked. The young people were hungry for social activity to break the routine of work in the cotton fields and were willing to tolerate the dissertation on fire and brimstone. There is a hazing custom, still extant in a few hill communities where the sexes are divided by a central aisle in church. The hazing is a matter of throwing rocks at a fellow who is bold enough to escort a girl home from church, provided he can be found and chased as he leaves the girl's home. The better the running, the fewer the hits.

The courthouse towns of agricultural counties offer the rural visitor a few advantages which are not based on an immediate *quid pro quo*. The courthouse and lawn or square around it may furnish space for coming and going, for sitting and talking, for a good neighborhood center. Such a center has become more important for the rural masses with the numerical reduction of country postoffices and justices of the peace, the development of better roads and transportation, and the increasing contact between citizens and government. At this center there is also likely to be a county farm agent, who is not a commercial exploiter and who has become important as the dispenser of government benefit checks to farmers. His social and political outlooks, however, are generally in closer tune with planters than with tenants. A later adjunct may be a relief or welfare authority. There is a distinct improvement in the appearance of the average rural courthouse as compared with former horse-and-buggy days. There is more grass in the yard and less tobacco stain on floors and in-

TOWNS AND VILLAGES

terior walls, and the building itself may have been overhauled through a public works project.

Country and village high schools as well as consolidated rural schools have brought greater possibilities for community centers and community leadership in the Southern region of many children. Besides serving as a center for children, the schools have community possibilities for adults, partly offsetting the loss of rural postoffices. The modern school expansion is, however, circumscribed by the South's limited school revenue and by the splitting of school funds as well as systems between two races. It is hard to envisage an effective community center developing through the inadequately housed and supported school for Negroes as found in the average rural district of the South.

The South has more towns with newspapers than any other section except the Western group of states extending from Iowa to Wyoming. Many of these Southern newspaper centers are relatively small towns and rural county seats. It is known that some of these country papers are paying properties, and the number of one-paper towns is not decreasing so rapidly as the number of two-paper or three-paper towns. County-seat newspapers particularly are holding their own from the standpoint of existence, but one might question whether they are keeping abreast of the trends of the times. They frequently display a deficiency in serving community needs, in presenting local and general news of social significance, and in participating effectively in enlightened public opinion. An editorial timidity tends to lurk between "boiler-plate" matter and advertisements, with a minimum of offense to local politics or to vested interests with local connections. There are refreshing exceptions, such as the venture of the Tupelo (Mississippi) *Journal* under the editorship of George McLean and, in some ways, the Crowley (Louisiana) *Signal*, the Anniston (Alabama) *Star*, and the Dothan (Alabama) *Eagle*. If there is a strong tendency toward editorial independency, the editor is likely to hear directly or indirectly from some corporate interest. There are confessions on this point.

The social unawareness of the rural press may be illustrated by reference to the Arkansas share cropper controversy. This burning problem became nationally important and nationally known with a minimum of attention by the press of that rural commonwealth. A Little Rock resident and writer said that for months after the issue made the national headlines he was unable to find a scrap of comment on the subject in any paper published in the state.

The rural South needs genuine country editors just as it needs country physicians. Of both classes there seems to be a real shortage. The wide circulation of the Southern agricultural press is an index of the rural demand for something to read on rural issues. This index may also point to the social opportunity for a country press. But if the first duty of the little town and its newspaper is the service of the surrounding open country on which they depend, the prevailing economy of the cotton belt tends to prevent that service and to make the town and the town paper antennae of the big city. The outlook is commercial and cityward. The little town hopes to be a city, just as the farmer perhaps hopes to be a business man or to send sons into business or the professions.

The up-country and border regions of the cotton belt contain market towns which surpass the one-crop towns in economic balance. They are surrounded by a diversified agriculture and a good proportion of independent farmers. Some of these centers came through the depression with a minimum of distress and bankruptcy. Farm diversification does not prevent any possible discrimination by the town against the countryside. But it tends to minimize exploitation by making farmers more able to live at home without reliance on the profit systems of the towns. It prevents any wide fluctuation in the farmer's real purchasing power between times of prosperity and depression. The farmers of multiple crops and interests have a bargaining power and a civic power not possessed by the general run of cotton tenants. Exceptions must be made of many isolated mountaineers, piney-woods men, and bayou dwellers, who receive fewer village blessings than share croppers.

The villages and towns surrounded and supported by diversified farming have much less enforced idleness than the cotton-farm centers, just as the diversified farmers have less than the cotton farmers. As a rank stranger, I could find much more of interest by spending a day of ob-

There are health-giving elements in Southern rural life which even ignorance and poverty cannot nullify.

A tenant family in their home in Alabama.   White tenants occupy what was once the "Big House."

The child of a North Carolina share cropper.   Share cropper's child clad in a tow sack.

Arkansas share cropper's child.   A Blue Ridge mountain boy, Virginia.

"THE MAJORITY OF SHARE-CROPPER FAMILIES HAVE A VERY LOW PLANE OF LIVING...."

TOWNS AND VILLAGES

servation in a farm town of East Tennessee than in the capital of Arkansas's greatest cotton producing county of the world. I have made the comparison. Cotton breeds monotony along with progress and poverty.

Every farm town and many a farm village is also something else, such as a political, educational or tourist center. Often the farmers' market place is also an industrial center, at least to a small extent. It is true and can not be too much emphasized that, in American economic development since the Civil War, industrial interests have, on the whole, had the advantage over agricultural interests. In other words, the business men who own and control American industries have been able to exercise a large degree of economic and political dominance in comparison with the power of farmers. Much of the time the industrialists have controlled national and governmental policy without regard to the interests of farmers. But the relationship between industrialists and farmers should not be confused, as so often is the case, with that between industry and agriculture.

It is important to differentiate between industrialism as an entrepreneur system and the physical process of industry or industrialization, which may be put at the service of all men, including farmers. Industry is good for agriculture, though the American industrialists may have denied American farmers a square deal. Industry furnishes the farmer a market, perchance at home, and makes it possible for him to have working equipment and physical comforts not otherwise obtainable. Industry furnishes an outlet for the growing surplus population of the farms, an item of vast importance to the South. Industry may make it possible for farmers to have a superior town and village system.

There is much to be condemned in the textile manufacturing towns of the South. The industrial masters of these centers have often exploited docile "Anglo-Saxon" labor, drawn from tenant classes and from independent farm families of the up-country. Southern textile workers come to the mill village with a minimum background of community interest and experience. They are unaccustomed to civic responsibility. Much of the paternalistic caste spirit of the plantation has characterized the typical mill village of the South, with the head of the mill taking the role of the planter. But the spread of the textile industry has served to cushion the economic collapse of cotton tenancy in the Southeast. It is hard to say or to prove that cotton tenants made their lot worse by moving to mill villages.

Farmers, in the large group sense, fare better and experience less market exploitation in industrial areas than in areas which are rather exclusively devoted to one-crop agriculture. On a drive from Asheville to Raleigh in North Carolina one is scarcely out of sight of an industrial town or village; but from Raleigh to Wilmington industrial centers are rare, and farm life, in spite of the potential productivity, is of a distinctly lower order than on the other stretch. Industrial villages may serve as the best agricultural villages. Professor R. P. Brooks, of the University of Georgia, has aptly pointed out in a study of Southern industrialization that a superior type of agriculture tends to prevail in those sub-regions where there is a high type of industrial development. This is true of the agriculture by both the economic and the scientific test.

The importance of agriculture in industrial-agricultural districts, or for towns supported by both agriculture and industry, is unfortunately minimized or somewhat ignored. Value added by the agricultural process, as in cotton or tobacco, gets swallowed up in the manufactured product, with the whole value credited to manufacturing by the town boosters, who comparatively overestimate their local industries and adopt a false industrial sophistication. This opens the way for advantages to the industrial rulers in legislative demands, taxation exemptions, labor relations, and other issues of policy. The town, in its industrial worship, fails properly to see and to serve the open country which gives it strength. This lopsidedness of perspective is the more likely where there is a large-scale and undiversified processing of cheap goods. A hick town with a single plant forgets it is a hick town, and large power falls to a steel, a textile, or a tobacco magnate in many parts of the agricultural South. For good or for ill, the head of the industry is head of the town. Main Street may be a reflection of Wall Street whether the Main Streeters are lowland planters or Appalachian industrialists.

The small town with a diversified economic life achieves something of

TOWNS AND VILLAGES

a social balance and tends to escape the concentration of power in too few private hands. In several ways it may serve the farmer better than the other type. Kingsport, in East Tennessee, has been praised as a town of diversified economy in a farm district. The coming of a railroad caused it to be transformed from an open field to an industrial center. A varied group of small plants was established, including a chemical plant, book bindery, tannery, hosiery mill, cement works, brick yard, and smaller enterprises, all employing laborers from the surrounding farms. As a result, Kingsport in the year of the depression, 1933, was reported to have raised its community chest quota by eleven o'-clock of the first day of the campaign.

The tillers of the soil, as distinguished from the important lords of the land, are likely to find more physical conveniences and attractions in the industrial town than in the strictly commercial one, for industrialists are aware of the importance of good will and morale on the part of labor and of voters. Such a town is more likely to have baseball, movies and other forms of amusement or welfare without denial to the farming class. An industrial payroll is also a stimulant to the purchases of certain types of farm products. Industrial taxes may go in part to the aid of farmers through roads and educational funds. Electrification may be made more available to farmers by the existence of industrial centers in the vicinity. But the unorganized farmers merely get pot-luck in Southern industrial or commercial centers except spasmodically when they get on the warpath.

Figuratively, there are few two-way streets of economic, social, and cultural relationships between Southern town-village centers and the open country. The rural trade centers have been or become instruments and victims of an unfair exchange between factory and farm. There are minor exceptions and major pronouncements, but a large problem is here for attack. Something can be done about it. What?

CHAPTER SIX

FARMS FOR FARMERS

THE STATUS OF FARMING AND OF RURAL SOCIETY IN THE SOUTH CALLS FOR public consideration and action. It is of vital public concern that the erosion of our beautiful hills be checked. It is important that all possible steps be taken to arrest the depletion of the soil, which Southerners love so much and likewise abuse so much. It is important for Southern and American civilization that hillbilly farmers produce more and get more and that their social life be elevated. The development of public responsibility for rural welfare requires sweeping changes in the Southern patterns of human relationships, including those between employers and employees, between landlords and tenants, and between citizens and their government. Certain changes are inevitable, either through resort to violence or through a constructive application of the democratic process. The South can choose the latter, but the South must choose.

There are parallel lines of approach which should be taken simultaneously if the South is to experience a rural renaissance. One approach would deal with national and local commercial policy in relationship to farmers. Another concerns industrial policy, rural or decentralized manufacturing, and the coördination between industry and agriculture. Still another concerns the coöperative distribution of social and political burdens between town and country. There are others. The most basic line of approach to Southern problems heads directly into the issues connected with land. Among these urgent land issues are those of ownership, tenure and policy.

FARMS FOR FARMERS

It is becoming slowly recognized that land is an essential social asset which should not remain an object of unlimited private speculation. Nation after nation throughout the world has been compelled to give public attention to the problems of land policy in the last fifty years. The demand for such attention has increased since the World War, affecting with equal force dictatorships and democracies, conservative and radical governments. Land reform was an important factor in the various postwar revolutions in Eastern Europe, including Russia. The organizers of the Russian Revolution seemingly utilized the experience of the French Revolution in making a successful appeal to peasants, for in both revolutions an important item was land for the landless.

The evolutionary land reforms in several countries of Western Europe during the last generation have appealed to many American students of rural problems as examples and experience which should be instructive for the United States, for the South. Our interest in foreign land policies has increased in the last few years with the increasing urgency of farm tenancy in the United States. L. C. Gray, government agricultural economist, Elwood Mead, reclamation engineer, and Clarence Poe, editor of *The Progressive Farmer*, are among the many leaders who have suggested American public action in the light of the democratic experience of other nations with respect to land policy. Poe has written and spoken extensively on the subject since a European visit for study and observation a quarter of a century ago. An abundance of documentary information on foreign land-tenure changes has been made available by different government agencies at Washington, especially by the Resettlement Administration.

Two countries in which the burden of farm tenancy was removed are Ireland and Denmark. Writing of them, Charles S. Johnson says, "The chief lessons in the experience of these countries are that (a) drastic agrarian reforms, aimed at converting tenants into owners, were finally and completely accepted as necessary; (b) these changes required the sympathetic and material aid of the State; (c) in each case the legislation had to be admittedly experimental, and was changed as unanticipated problems presented themselves; (d) in each case the experiment began in doubt about the ability of the tenant farmer to carry into and sustain himself in ownership; and (e) in each case it has been revealed that the mentality of the tenant has been the result of his status rather than that his status has been a result of his mentality."

Ireland was parallel to the South in the development of farm tenancy and the absentee ownership of plantations, with political complications which were different from Southern politics. Protective legislation for tenants began under the British ministry of Gladstone in 1870. Continued tenant agitation led to the formulation in 1879 of an Irish Land League under the leadership of Michael Davitt. An official Land Commission was created in 1881. Improvement of tenant conditions and terms was followed by land purchase acts with provision for government aid. Under an act of 1903 the British government advanced to many thousands of Irish tenants the full purchase price of land with provision for repayments in sixty-eight and a half annual installments of three and a half per cent, including one-half per cent sinking fund. The government of the Irish Free State took still more sweeping steps to turn tenants into owners under the guidance of the powerful Land Commission. Since 1871 over 400,000 Irish farmers have been assisted in the purchase of land. Land profiteering has been kept down, and there have been notable improvements in farm roads, fences and livestock. In spite of the severe political and economic troubles of recent years, the face of the Irish countryside is changing, attractive cottages are supplanting huts, and farm families are able to raise their standard of living.

Major legislation for small agricultural holdings took place in Denmark in 1899, followed by similar legislation in Norway and Sweden. Denmark, once tenant-ridden, was well on the road to farmer ownership when this step was taken. Much had already been done through a century of legislative measures for the improvement of agriculture and the reduction of tenancy. The farmers had been using their votes and had been forming coöperative societies for such functions as credit, buying, selling, processing, and stock-breeding. There were more than a thousand of these societies. Most of the farms were comparatively small, the average being about fifty acres. Through coöperative action the small farmers

FARMS FOR FARMERS

were gaining for themselves much of the efficiency and many of the economies of the large estates. But there were thousands of rural cottagers who had no farm land or not enough on which to make a living. Many of them were going to cities or to America to escape the hard work, low wages, and poor comforts of their native communities. This exodus was disturbing to the larger farmers and the nobles and made it possible for the voting cottagers by good leadership to start a government land program through the Act of 1899.

This law, primarily for the benefit of farm laborers, provided for state loans for the purchase and equipping of small farms. Subsequent acts have extended the program to other rural laborers. Provision was also made for locating small farmers on state lands on a tenure basis approximating possession without technical ownership. Settlers on these lands might borrow money for improvements. The loans have been for a maximum of ninety per cent of the value of the property. The interest rates have ranged from three to four and a half per cent per year. No payment on principal is required for the first five years, and the amortization schedule may be extended over ninety-three years. Loans are also made to combinations of farmers. Annual appropriations have permitted an expansion of the program, which has already been applied to more than 20,000 farmers and gardeners, a substantial number for so small a country.

The Danish aid plan has been worked through national, county and local agencies or committees. The plan requires actual farming, improvement and maintenance on the part of the settler. Sale, transfer or mortgage of a farmer's equity is restricted in various ways. "These restrictions," says Elizabeth R. Hooker, "are intended to safeguard the financial investment of the State, prevent speculation, eliminate applicants unlikely to be good citizens and good farmers, and ensure the permanence of each small holding as a unit capable of affording adequate support for a family." This public action on the relationship between man and the land in Denmark has improved agricultural productivity. It has eased the rural population problem, though it has not removed that problem. The growth of farm ownership has combined with educational improvement

FORTY ACRES AND STEEL MULES

and the coöperative movement to make rural life and living worth while in Denmark.*

The public sponsorship of farm ownership in England, Australia and other countries might be reviewed for profitable suggestions. The situation differs in different countries, but wherever land settlement has become a public responsibility, the advances or credits carry a low interest rate, varying from two and a half to five per cent, and allow a repayment period varying from twenty to ninety years.

The most successful experience in the public development of farm ownership has been on the basis of a somewhat careful selection of applicants and farms for the program, with emphasis on the adaptability of the men and the land for agriculture. Character and acquaintance with the soil are important requirements. Staking urban industrial workers to farm properties is generally considered risky, unless they are very young or previously were farmers or farm workers. It is recognized that success in farming requires habits and experience not to be acquired by townsmen reading books. The will to farm is not enough to make a farmer. "Men may be born fools or poets," it has been said, "but farmers, never." It takes education, practical experience, and hard work to make a farmer. The public promotion of small-scale part-time farming for industrial workers in rural areas has had a measure of success. But land settlement offers no direct solution of the major problems of urban unemployment.**

It is significant to note that governments which have adopted land policies with public aid to worthy farmers have assumed that providing land is not enough for success in agriculture. Pioneer days are over, even in America, which no longer has a general frontier country. Land and

* Miss Hooker's study, *Recent Policies Designed to Promote Farm Ownership in Denmark* (Resettlement Administration, Land Use Planning Publication No. 15, March, 1937) is a valuable document on the workings of the Danish government program. See also M. W. Childs, *Sweden: The Middle Way* (New Haven, 1936), ch. x; F. C. Howe, *Denmark: The Co-operative Way* (New York, 1936); and Elwood Mead, *Helping Men Own Farms* (New York, 1920).

** Erich Kraemer, *Selection of Settlers in Agricultural Settlement of Several European Countries* (Resettlement Administration, Land Use Planning Publication No. 5, July, 1936).

Evans — The cost of this wagon was effort only. It has wooden axles, wheels, and pins. Dixon's Mill Community, Marengo County, Alabama.

FSA Lange — An ox team hauling pulp wood in Mississippi. This method of transportation is not uncommon in the region.

FSA Lange — The South is a land of contrasts, perhaps no greater than in other regions, but more closely juxtaposed.

FSA Rothstein — "Thousands of Southern participants in the program of 1934 had to make crops with oxen as the only work animals."

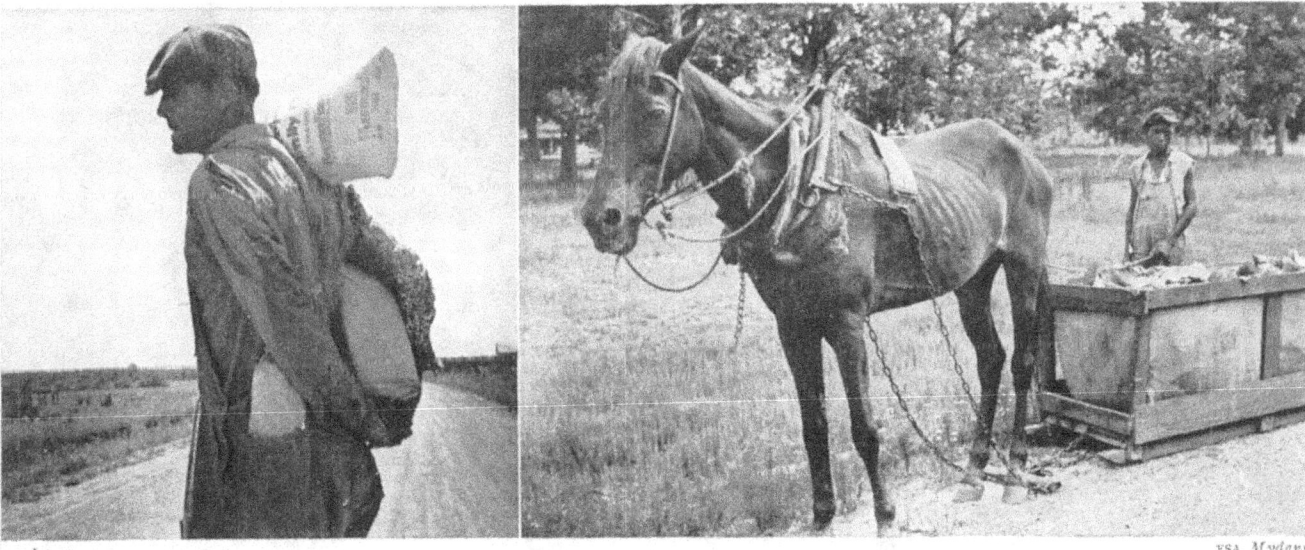

FSA Lange — A common method of transportation even on main-traveled highways.

FSA Mydans — Tobacco starts, in a homemade sled, on its long and picturesque career.

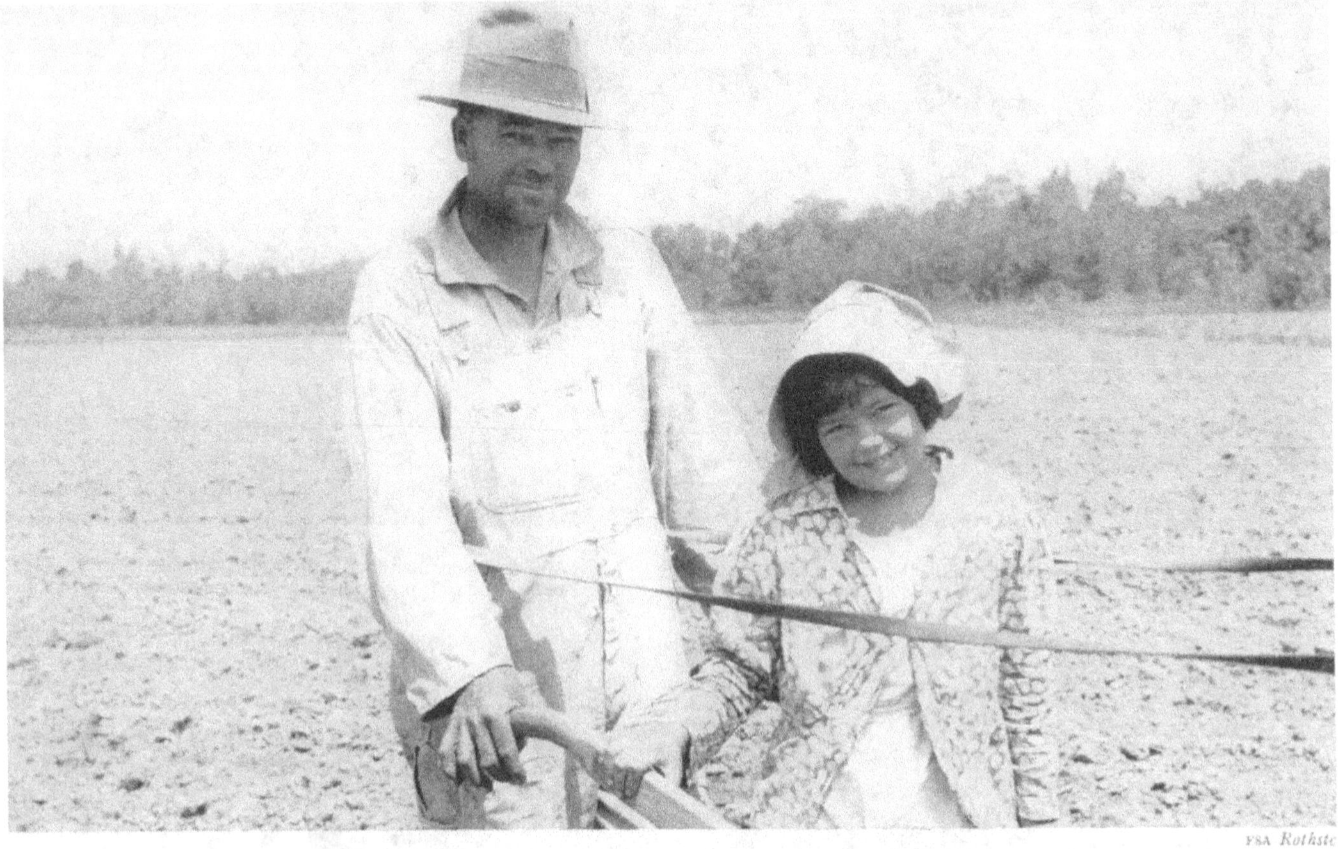

FSA Rothste

Rehabilitation client and his daughter on a cotton cultivator in Arkansas.

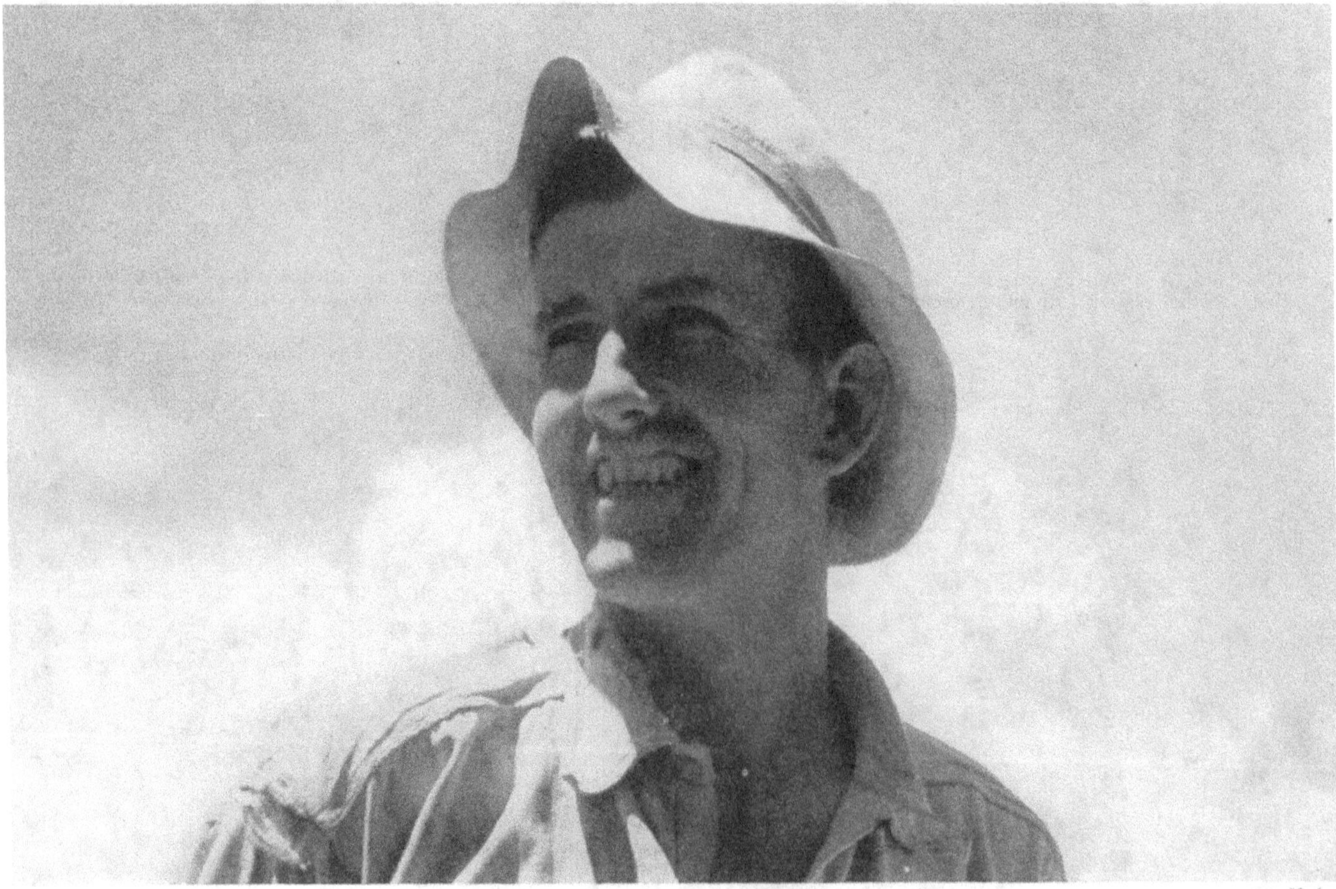

FSA Mydan

A young "resettled" farmer in Arkansas.

FARMS FOR FARMERS

labor are no longer enough for farming. There should be capital enough or credit enough for a farmer to have or acquire the essential implements, livestock, seeds, plants, trees, and buildings. It is also true that farmers' cash incomes are small, and that the rate of return on their investment is small. Hence the advances for their initial capital, as with advances for land purchase, must carry a low rate of interest and be repaid gradually. Such a procedure is as applicable to the South as to Denmark or Ireland, if the ills of farm tenancy are to be reduced.

Efforts have been made in the last several years to center American public attention on the problem of land policy and farm tenancy, which is so acute in the South. When the Federal Land Bank system was provided for in 1916, Clarence Poe, with his European studies in mind, sought to have it made "more emphatically an aggressive agency for converting tenants into home owners." The system, as established, could not accommodate agricultural workers, typical Southern tenants, or other little fellows, who would have to start from scratch. It has required in each case a land value security substantially in excess of the amount of the loan. It has been, at least for the South, something of a landlord's bank, though it approaches foreign examples of low interest and long terms. Farm relief in the nineteen-twenties embraced congressional and administrative measures for intermediate credit and commodity loans, including aid to coöperatives. The New Deal's consolidated Farm Credit Administration provides for these features and others, including seed loans, the refinancing of farm mortgages, scaling down obligations, and reducing interest rates. Less heralded than the crop control measures of the government, this program of cheaper credit is significant as a factor contributing to the real income of those farmers who can participate in the system. Most of the share tenants and croppers of the Southeast can benefit by these credit measures only indirectly through their landlords.

Different land settlement plans were officially proposed between the end of the World War and the beginning of the Great Depression. The state of California in 1917 started a homestead experiment with long-period, low-interest loans to a small community of farmers, providing for nearly all the cost of the land and a large part of the cost of buildings and equipment. There was a Bankhead colonization bill before Congress in 1921, and subsequent bills in the twenties. In 1926 the Interior Department, with the aid of a small congressional appropriation, made an investigation of opportunities for land reclamation and planned group settlement in the Southern states, especially in the Southeast. The committee appointed to make this survey consisted of Howard Elliott, railway official and president of the Harvard Board of Overseers, Daniel C. Roper, the present secretary of Commerce, and George Soule, editor of *The New Republic*. Elwood Mead, author of *Helping Men Own Farms,* and others aided them. They visited the farm colonies near Wilmington, North Carolina, which had been developed by Hugh MacRae and which will be considered in the next chapter. They looked over prospective sites for land settlement in the Carolinas, Georgia, Alabama, Mississippi and Tennessee. They went into such questions as tenancy, indebtedness, abandoned farms, and the one-crop system. They noted that in the South there were available at low prices fine lands which could be used for the development of model settlements under the joint sponsorship of national, state and local governments. Incidentally they suggested a smaller per capita acreage and a more intensive cultivation than is the practice in the South. They pointed out that a needed expansion in the Southern diet would increase consumption sufficiently to keep pace with an increase in the region's food production for a good period of time. On the general problem of land settlement their report contained the following statement:

"The experience of the United States and of other countries has led to a new view of reclamation. Reclamation is not complete when engineering works have been constructed, but only when successful and happy farming communities are established on the land reclaimed. The establishment of such communities requires sufficiently low prices for land; easy purchase terms on an amortized basis; preparation of the farms for cultivation before the arrival of settlers; adequate capital or credit for improvements, implements, and supplies; an agricultural program expertly prepared in advance of settlement;

FARMS FOR FARMERS

careful choice of settlers; guidance of the colony after its start; proper economic organization; provision of community facilities."

Land issues came to the forefront in the depression, which reversed the cityward drift of population and brought for the first time in many years a net migration to the country. This situation and the general market conditions intensified attention to subsistence farming, land settlement and rural rehabilitation. The state of New York worked out a program of rural land planning under the governorship of Franklin D. Roosevelt, who showed real interest in the movement, explaining it with enthusiasm, for instance, at the University of Virginia Institute of Public Affairs in 1931.

The AAA crop program of 1933-35 reduced tenant mobility and limited tenancy expansion in basic crop areas in the face of the population movement to the country. Moreover, the cotton set-up of the AAA was more favorable to landlords than to relatively inarticulate tenants. It had to favor the landlords, who had political power, if it was to be adopted and put into practice. It was natural that tenant issues and complaints should come to a crisis in areas where both cotton acreage and tenancy had been rapidly expanding in recent years, as in Arkansas. Expanding relief rolls called additional attention to stranded rural families. It was a condition which confronted the Roosevelt administration, not a theory.

The creation of the TVA was one answer, a long-run regional answer to the problem of hillbilly poverty. A step, directed more immediately at the emergency, was the provision for subsistence homesteads in the following section of the National Industrial Recovery Act:

"To provide for aiding the redistribution of the overbalance of population in industrial centers $25,000,000 is hereby made available to the President, to be used by him through such agencies as he may establish and under such regulations as he may make, for making loans for and otherwise aiding in the purchase of subsistence homesteads. The moneys collected as repayment of said loans shall constitute a revolving fund to be administered as directed by the President for the purposes of this section."

FORTY ACRES AND STEEL MULES

The administration of this activity was by the Division of Subsistence Homesteads of the Department of the Interior until it was taken over by the newer Resettlement Administration. M. L. Wilson was in charge of the division for a time, and the work was started with the assumed purpose of developing a permanent policy of dealing with stranded population groups, such as those in abandoned mine communities, in cut-over timber regions, and on eroded farms. The South was highly eligible for aid under these aims and under a point stressed in a divisional circular of November 15, 1933, which said, "full consideration will be given to demonstration projects for Negroes and other racial groups" and added that the "impact of the depression in both agriculture and industry has been particularly severe upon the Negro." About a third of the undertakings were located in the South.

The Federal Relief Administration was able to devote more funds and more effort to a rural program than was the Subsistence Homestead Division. With hundreds of thousands of rural clients requiring relief, this agency launched a large program of rural rehabilitation under the direction of Colonel Lawrence Westbrook, a former planter of Texas. The general features of the plan were set forth at a regional conference in Atlanta in March, 1934, with Harry Hopkins present to pledge scores of millions of dollars for a new day for distressed farm families of the South. It was an inspiration to attend this conference. One planter delegate assured Mr. Hopkins that it was the greatest blessing offered the South by the national government in the years since the Civil War.

This rural rehabilitation program in the South applied largely to share tenants or croppers and farm laborers, including stranded families who formerly made their living by one of these methods. A percentage of farm owners came into the scheme, some of them for removal from poor lands to more productive tracts. A limited amount of coöperative enterprise, rural industry, and community building was scheduled. Supervised or community canning of fruits and vegetables was a significant feature of the program. This resulted in canning by many families who had never canned before.

The most extensive work connected with this program, however, was

FARMS FOR FARMERS

the transfer of farm families from pure relief to a rehabilitated status on a basis of supervised tenancy rather than of actual ownership. The financial aid for these tenants was timely and improved the rural morale. It was on a contractual basis, and substantial repayments have been made by rural clients who got on their feet. The plan had many shortcomings. It had to be worked out hurriedly and changed in many details with red tape complications. Drought conditions intensified the picture. The funds were too limited for a genuine reconstruction in view of the excessive number of rural families needing aid. Thousands of Southern participants in the program in 1934 had to make crops with oxen as the only work animals. Serious attention had to be given to so many families at or below the bottom rung of the agricultural ladder that little effort could be given toward elevating families who might already be a rung or two above the bottom. Definite emphasis had to be placed on subsistence farming, and there were great difficulties in making arrangements for suitable lands with AAA quotas for basic cash crops. Subsistence farming with inadequate capital or equipment or cash crops suggested the danger of perpetuating poverty.

This plan, however, justified its existence as a rural work program under the difficult circumstances. Most of this work was taken over and expanded by the Resettlement Administration, which also became the agency for handling other rural and village projects. After functioning about two years as an independent establishment under the direction of Rexford Tugwell, the Resettlement Administration, with W. W. Alexander, a Southerner, as its new head, was transferred to the Department of Agriculture and subsequently changed in name to the Farm Security Administration.

The landlord-tenant controversies in Arkansas, Alabama, and elsewhere in the cotton section continued to bring national attention to the ills of tenancy, and it became clear to many that the available agencies and funds were inadequate. Extensive study and investigation led to the formulation of the Bankhead-Jones farm tenant bill in 1935. This bill was designed to translate worthy tenants, croppers and farm laborers into landowning farmers under government financial sponsorship with low rates of interest and long terms for payment. It provided for the ultimate use of a billion dollars for the undertaking. It passed the Senate, but a legislative jam prevented its coming to a vote in the house. The South, with so many farmers to be touched by the program, was strikingly apathetic, with the exception of a few articulate groups and voices.

The discussion of the tenant problem and the work for the Bankhead-Jones bill served to attract the attention of many newspapers and political leaders, including Secretary Wallace and President Roosevelt. Correction of the ills of tenancy became one of the cards of the New Deal in the campaign of 1936. Soon after the election, the President appointed a committee on farm tenancy, embracing experts and publicists. The committee arranged five regional hearings, two of them in the South, at Montgomery, Alabama, and Dallas, Texas. The Southern situation was well recognized in the committee's report, which was prepared by L. C. Gray, John D. Black, E. G. Nourse, A. G. Black, Charles S. Johnson, Lowry Nelson, W. W. Alexander, and M. W. Thatcher.

The report was transmitted to Congress on February 16, 1937. It noted that farmers are insecure because of their disproportionately small share of the national income and because of a faulty distribution of this share. It recommended further that the national administration undertake to improve land leasing for farmers, extend credit aid to indebted small farmers, and expand the Resettlement Administration's work of rural rehabilitation and removal of farmers from sub-marginal lands. It urged attention to improvement in the conditions of farm laborers, who, in general, "have not shared in the benefits of either Federal or State legislation providing for collective bargaining; unemployment, accident, and old-age insurance; and requirements for assuring safe and sanitary conditions of employment."

The report recommended that the states adopt concomitant "measures to improve lease contracts and landlord-tenant relationships; to modify taxation of farm lands; and to safeguard the civil liberties of tenants." Referring to recent organizations of tenants, croppers, and farm laborers to increase bargaining power, it urged that these groups be effectively protected by the states as to the rights of peaceful assembly and of organization. The committee in these remarks was venturing with caution into important but controversial questions. Civil or human rights for insecure tenants constitute an old problem, a problem known in other countries and other ages but intensified in the South because of race and the small voting power of Negroes. It is not easy for Southern planters to consent gracefully to collective bargaining for share croppers.

It is important to note individual statements by three Southern members of the President's committee. Charles S. Johnson said that the decentralizing features should be accompanied by safeguards to insure the inclusion in the benefits of Negro tenants and croppers. W. L. Blackstone, representing the Southern Tenant Farmers' Union on the committee, objected to putting the Federal aid program under the Department of Agriculture, because it would mean too much domination by rich or large landowning farmers. He dissented from the "small homestead" philosophy and desired more emphasis on coöperative activity. He wanted a stronger statement on civil liberties, which should not be left entirely as a matter for the states. He expressed genuine approval of the proposals to prevent beneficiaries from disposing of equities to speculators or landgrabbers. Edward A. O'Neal, Alabamian and president of the American Farm Bureau Federation, strongly dissented, as a member of the committee, from these particular provisions which Blackstone praised. Here was a cleavage between the representatives of big farmers and the champion of small farmers and tenants. The successful Danish practice is in line with the Blackstone view, but O'Neal opposed such social control "as contrary to sound American jurisprudence."

The important report was referred to the House Committee on Agriculture, which considerably emasculated the proposals and seemingly fell in line with the O'Neal point of view, favoring a policy for granting farm loans without restrictions or control features to check or prevent speculation. A Farm Security Act was passed by the House, but, after delay, was changed in the Senate to conform in slight part with the recommendations of the President's Committee. Because of a legislative jam and the emphasis on a budget-balancing economy, Secretary Wallace and others soon concluded that there was little hope for substantial farm tenure legislation at this time. As finally worked out in conference committee and passed, the bill contained barriers to limit speculation for a period of five years in each instance, and it opened the way for a degree of expert farm supervision. It really established a loan policy, rather than a land policy, and it gave local county committees the power to pass on the man and the land for each loan. It provided for a total sum of eighty-five million dollars to be used in the program over the next three years, stepping the appropriation up to an annual amount of fifty millions within that period. The bill also authorized appropriations for the retirement of sub-marginal lands and a continuation of rural rehabilitation work. As the lands farmed in the United States by tenants are worth several billions of dollars, it must be said that this action is a moderate step. It can not offset the annual tenant increases unless there is a let-up in tenancy growth. It represents, however, a distinct recognition of the problem. It may be improved and expanded through the years, as has been the case with land legislation in other countries.*

Significant for the South should be Secretary Wallace's recent observation that the Department of Agriculture has heretofore been concerned primarily with the top third of American farmers, and that it must henceforth turn attention to the others. The lower two-thirds in the South need land, they need organization, and they need community life.

* It is possible for a healthy administration to offset in a measure the imperfections of this legislation. The work of the Farm Security Administration was put into sympathetic hands with W. W. Alexander as its head.

FSA Lange

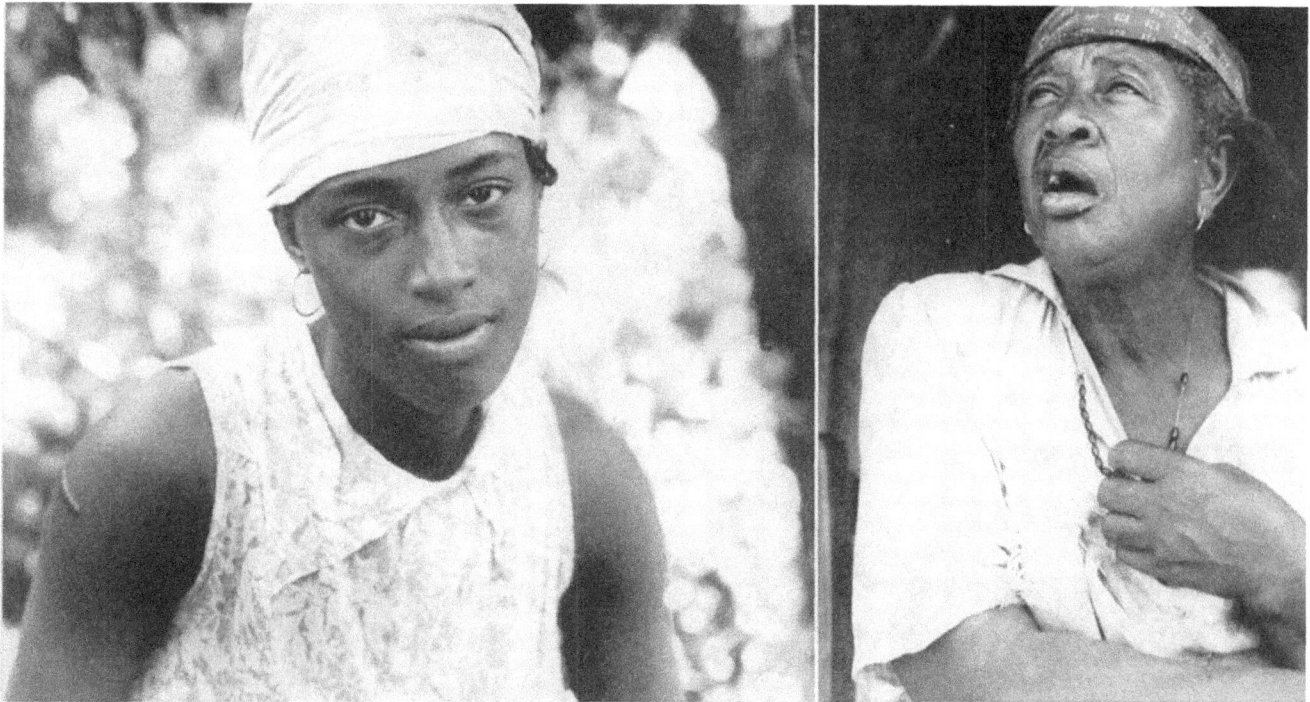

A cotton hoer near Clarksdale, Mississippi.

FSA Lange

A share-cropper woman of Hinds County, Mississippi. She wears black beads to prevent heart trouble.

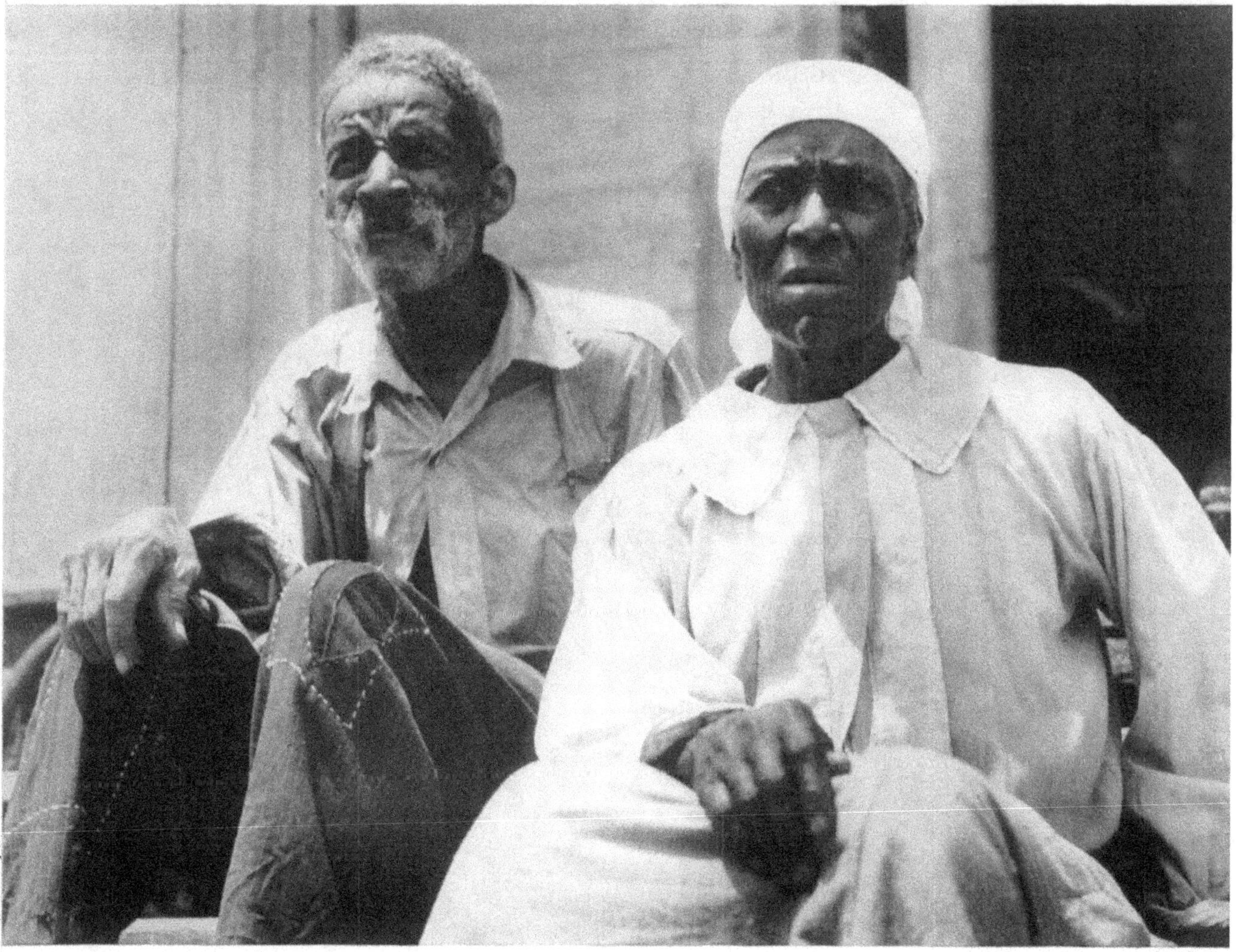

FSA Lange

An ex-slave and his wife, tenants in a Georgia plantation house now in decay.

HAVE YOU REALLY SEEN THEIR FACES?

FSA *Lange*
Truck-load of cotton hoers from Memphis.

FSA *Lange*
A plow boy in Alabama, who earns seventy-five cents a day.

FSA *Rothstein*
One of the tenants at Gee's Bend, Alabama.

FSA *Lange*
Children at the Delta Coöperative Farm, Hillhouse, Mississippi.

"NEGROES FURNISH GOOD HUMAN MATERIAL FOR ORGANIZATION AND COÖPERATION,..."

CHAPTER SEVEN

VILLAGES FOR VILLAGERS

FARM OWNERSHIP OR A SOUNDER LEASE POLICY IS NOT ENOUGH TO ENABLE Southern hillbillies to live in decency. It is essential to provide by public effort for social and economic coöperation among small farmers, to make possible a better system of farm villages. It might be said that we should endeavor to recapture the community spirit of the past. Our pioneers on the rural frontier, with all their emphasized individualism, practiced a material and social coöperation, which has been displaced and obscured by a subsequent urban dominance over the economy of the countryside. House-raisings, log-rollings, and corn-shuckings exemplified coöperative labor on the part of good neighbors. Little communities frequently centered around one-room schools or churches, cross-road stores, fourth-class postoffices, and picturesque water mills. These little societies were examples of informal coöperation and had something of the organic flavor which Sir Henry Maine attributed to the "ancient Teutonic cultivating communities."

Many of these single-cell community centers have passed away under the influence of consolidated schools, rural free delivery of mail, large-scale production and commerce, and an enlarged transportation radius. In many instances there have been no real substitutes for these natural but incidental centers. The prevailing farm neighborhood in the South today is little more than an aggregation of individuals or families living in physical proximity and constituting a "geographic expression" rather than a real community. Rural life in the South is often dull because it is unorganized and isolated. The inhabitants have an outlook which is directed toward a city or big town rather than toward a home community center, and those who lack urban contact are socially stranded or submerged. It is pertinent to consider taking the small town or village to the country instead of compelling the countrymen to choose between living in isolation or going to the city or the big town. The cause of rural progress, in many ways, depends on the fortune of the small town.

Farm villages have developed less in the cotton South than in the North and less in the United States than in Europe. W. A. Terpenning makes factual and observational comparisons of American and European rural life in his important study, *Village and Open-Country Neighborhoods*. He finds more social life and coöperation, more physical comforts, and a higher type of civilization in villages than in the open country. He describes with touches of enthusiasm the sample villages selected from different countries. He praises the village life of Russia. He gives an intimate picture of a Swiss village of sixty families, where forty families own all the land they work and where running water in the home, electricity, and good fuel lighten the work of housekeeping. It is a compact village; the average distance from home to farm is not more than one kilometer, and the largest holding is the mayor's fifty hectares, while the smallest is little more than a garden spot. Denmark, Germany, and other countries furnish Terpenning striking examples of rural village life and coöperation. Many other writers have studied and admired Western European villages and village coöperation, especially in the Scandinavian countries. Mexican village life is also significant. That nation in its recent reform movement for the break-up of large plantations, has recognized the importance of the village in the life of small-scale proprietary farmers. The states of Mexico have assumed the function of creating zones around villages exclusively for small holdings.

The recent slackening in the dynamic growth of American cities and the partial shutting off of escape from the country to giant industrial centers give a new emphasis to the rural village, where inhabitants henceforth may find it necessary to brighten the corner where they are and to

VILLAGES FOR VILLAGERS

take their stand against exploitation by distant economic forces. The village, in reality, is an epitome of establishment and slowness of change. The slowing up of population growth and also of the demand for industrial labor may make the village the prevailing unit of the future. The ideal village is one owned and controlled by the villagers, and the South has the physical and human makings for an abundance of such villages. But the South has a serious problem of absentee ownership or control, which frequently stands in the way of a development of villages for villagers.

There are several instances in the South of experiments in planned villages and coöperative community development. Among the pre-depression examples are Fairhope, Alabama, the colony of New Llano in Louisiana, and the settlements sponsored by Hugh MacRae near Wilmington, North Carolina. The Fairhope village of fifteen hundred inhabitants is located on ground fronting Mobile Bay. It was started in 1904 by a group of reformers, some of whom had been disillusioned and disappointed in Iowa politics. The life and policy of the town are largely dominated by the Fairhope Single Tax Corporation, which has a hundred members and a large number of lessees and controls the central portion of the land area of the town, as well as several thousand acres outside. The corporation handles all tax problems and burdens on a single-tax basis and seeks to prevent individual speculation in real estate. Several coöperative mercantile enterprises have been discontinued, but light and water utilities are owned and operated by the municipality. Founded by a group from other regions, the colony has not attracted Alabamians and embraces no Negroes in its population. The little state bank of Fairhope was the one bank in its county to escape depression trouble. It was not burdened with land paper. The center is rather free from tumble-down shacks, and its stores are neat. It is noted for a school of organic education, which has been under the direction of Mrs. Marietta Johnson for many years. It has annual Shakespeare plays by local talent in an outdoor theatre and unusual musical programs.

The Llano colony was founded in California more than twenty years ago and transferred three years later to Louisiana as New Llano. It represents an experiment in production coöperation in industrial and agricultural enterprise. It was organized on a share basis, with provision for optional community services and activities. It has had a large degree of self-sufficiency, and it survived the depression, after a fashion, in spite of poor land, lawsuits and secessions. The cult of bigness and the launching of industrial enterprises on borrowed money are contributing factors which recently put the affairs of the colony into a receivership. New Llano lacks the security and contentment of Fairhope.*

There are a few farm colonies near Wilmington, North Carolina, which have been developed under the scientific guidance and financial aid of Hugh MacRae and which were considered the "most impressive demonstration of what is possible in the South" by a visiting committee of the Department of the Interior in 1926. This committee found organized groups of happy and prosperous farmers carrying on an intensive and diversified cultivation of lands on which formerly were grown inferior crops of cotton. Few of these farmers had more than twenty acres and most of them were out of debt. Many of them were selected in Western Europe by Mr. MacRae many years ago, with the view of making effective demonstrations of community development, scientific farming with a large degree of subsistence, and successful coöperation. The founder has been pleased with the results, which include escape from tenancy and the one-crop system, keeping the soil in productive use the whole year round, and a nearly self-sustaining basis for each family in the matter of food, each having a cow, a vegetable garden and chickens. The experiments have distinctly tended to raise wages in the region and to influence the surrounding natives toward a better agriculture. One individual example of economic success is striking. "Less than ten years ago," says the report of the committee of 1926, "a Hollander who had been working in a laundry in New York City for $18 a week appeared at Wilmington with a capital of $300 and wanted to buy a farm. He was some-

---

* These colonies have attracted wide attention on the part of observers of experimental communities. They are given favorable treatment, for instance, by Charles Gide in his *Community and Co-operative Colonies* (New York, 1930) which first appeared as a French work in 1928 and which emphasizes that such village undertakings have been more successful than is generally assumed.

VILLAGES FOR VILLAGERS

what reluctantly accepted as a settler. Today he is worth at least $50,000. This accumulation is not invested in additional land, though of course the value of his original holding has greatly increased. This farmer has, in addition to building up his own farm, become president of a coöperative marketing association which now extends from the Virginia border into South Carolina."

The colonies developed by MacRae originally included a group of Italians at St. Helena, Dutch at Van Eeden, Germans at New Berlin, Poles and Ruthenians at Marathon, and a mixed group of Americans, Dutch, Hungarians, and Poles at Castle Hayne. About seventeen of the forty families at Castle Hayne became interested in bulbs and flowers. Other crops here include lettuce, snap-beans, English peas, corn, forage, and winter clover crops. Vegetable shipments have run into hundreds of cars per season. No cotton is grown. A high quality of truck farming is carried on, and the crops are disposed of through coöperative marketing associations composed of all farmers in the group. It seems that all have fared well except the Italians who met difficulties a few years after getting started, as prohibition legislation terminated their wine-making and grape culture.

MacRae has for many years been sponsoring and preaching the idea of encouraging small-scale intensive farming through demonstration communities. He has long felt that a sprinkling of such communities in the different states would revolutionize Southern agriculture and harmonize with a constructive program for the reduction of farm acreage by a plan of reforestation. But his twenty years or more of experimenting with farm communities convince him that the magnitude of the work is too great for private initiative alone and that government activity, state and national, must be brought into such undertakings.

Experiments in village planning and community coöperation have been undertaken by different government agencies since 1933 in connection with relief and resettlement. The last and most important of these agencies, as noted in the preceding chapter, is the Farm Security Administration, which has taken over much of the work of other agencies. The TVA and other authorities, however, continue a collateral interest in village development. Many of the villages or colonies have been planned and developed on an agricultural basis without reliance on extensive urban or industrial employment for income for the colonists. This has been particularly true in the South. The Dyess colony, near Osceola, Arkansas, for instance, is located on 20,000 acres in the heart of the most productive cotton area. Its several hundred white frame cottages, made partly from timber cut on the tract, shelter families whose living must come largely from the soil and whose cash income largely depends on cotton. The Cumberland homestead colony near Crossville, in East Tennessee, besides constructing cottages of native stone, produced an excellent market supply of potatoes in its first year under the direction of F. O. Clark, an agriculturalist with Berea College training. The Penderlea colony, about forty miles from Wilmington, North Carolina, was started with Hugh MacRae as project manager for a time and with the view of expanding the intensive and coöperative farming which had proved successful among the earlier and smaller colonies sponsored by MacRae. The Wooklake colony, near Houston, Texas, had 140 families busy growing vegetables in 1934 and canning them in a community plant. It early had a coöperative dairy and a work center for making furniture. This colony was planned essentially for subsistence farming and for coöperative industrial employment as the means of bringing in cash income. Other rural village and community projects in the South have been sponsored by government authorities. In most of them both landownership and coöperative endeavor have been stressed. Interesting reports on coöperative development have come from the Pine Mountain experiment near Warm Springs, Georgia. Here ten thousand acres were taken over for a combination of farming and industry with a plan for the community to produce seventy per cent of its total requirements within itself. It has been planned for scuppernong grapes to constitute an important cash crop. The farm units in this experimental community range from a few acres to forty.

These government-aided village projects represent a beginning of public responsibility for the community life of small farmers. They are worthy undertakings, and it is interesting to visit them and to contrast

VILLAGES FOR VILLAGERS

them with the planless life of Southern farm tenants. In place of a plantation mansion, there is a community center, which belongs to all. It must be said, however, that these projects have been started generally with rather heavy burdens of bureaucratic control, expensive overheads, and high construction costs. The individual farmers or the community must face future payments that are too much for them or the sponsoring government must take a technical loss.* It might be suggested that in some cases the aid and direction have been too exclusively from Washington and that the partnership of state and local governments might well be brought into the picture. There have been political difficulties in the way of going full steam ahead with coöperative economic enterprise, particularly in non-agricultural activity.

The Delta Coöperative Farm at Hillhouse, Mississippi, just south of Memphis, is a privately supported venture in share-cropper coöperation. On it thirty families were settled in 1936, and they were organized both as a producers' and a consumers' coöperative. Among the moving spirits in getting it under way were Sherwood Eddy, Dr. W. R. Amberson, formerly of the University of Tennessee, Howard Kester, and Sam Franklin, who became its director. Three of these four are ministers, and a missionary zeal has characterized their activity to convert evicted or stranded share croppers into a group of happy farmers. They have taken members of both races. Two thousand acres of land were purchased, and government aid was secured for malaria control and for making a road. Much of the land had to be cleared, and houses had to be constructed of lumber sawed from the timber. Recognizing the trend toward large-scale mechanized farming, the colony has made use of tractors, a cotton-picker, and expert advice. It reported a gross sale of cotton and lumber of $18,516.98 for 1936 and a net income of $9,587.62. This was in spite of a late start and an unfortunate drought. The director was able to appear before one of the government tenant hearings and speak

* It seems wise and fair that the government take a technical loss on these projects, which represented constructive spending for needed employment in hard times. The experiments should be treated as social investments, not as strictly "self-liquidating" projects. Share croppers and relief clients can not be "self-liquidated" into a status of good living and prosperity.

with eloquent enthusiasm on the first year of this farm community coöperative, which Sherwood Eddy describes under the pamphlet title, *A Door of Opportunity*. The founders hope to expand their efforts into a series of coöperative farms for needy families. Of this Eddy says, "The very economic success of our first project places upon us a larger responsibility to open more projects among these eight million destitute people."

This Mississippi experiment does not have the advantage of the best land of the delta region. But it may offer government planning authorities an example of high productivity and farmer income in proportion to investment and administrative costs. It is a test of the advantages of unrestricted coöperation for "dirt" farmers who are closer to the Southern Tenant Farmers' Union than to the American Farm Bureau Federation or to the American Cotton Coöperative Association. Its managerial cost is reduced by a philanthropic support, which can not be universally repeated.

These experimental villages and coöperative communities can furnish occupation and livelihood for only a very small proportion of the South's actual farmers and rural workers. There is a total capacity for only a few thousand families in all villages or projects of the types described in this chapter. But in the cotton states there are more than 100,000 rural families of very low incomes. The Farm Security Administration, through its rural rehabilitation activities, has been in touch with more than 50,000 families south of North Carolina and east of Texas, and there are thousands in rural poverty not touched by this agency. There are many other thousands who are not in economic want but who are victims of isolation. There are still other thousands earning a monotonous living in farm villages and hamlets which could be improved in economic status and community spirit by an application of the principles of coöperation. More serious than the economic backwardness in isolated areas is the denial of opportunity for education and creative expression to many worthy boys and girls.

The community needs of the South require that the timid experiments of the government should yield to a bold policy of farm village develop-

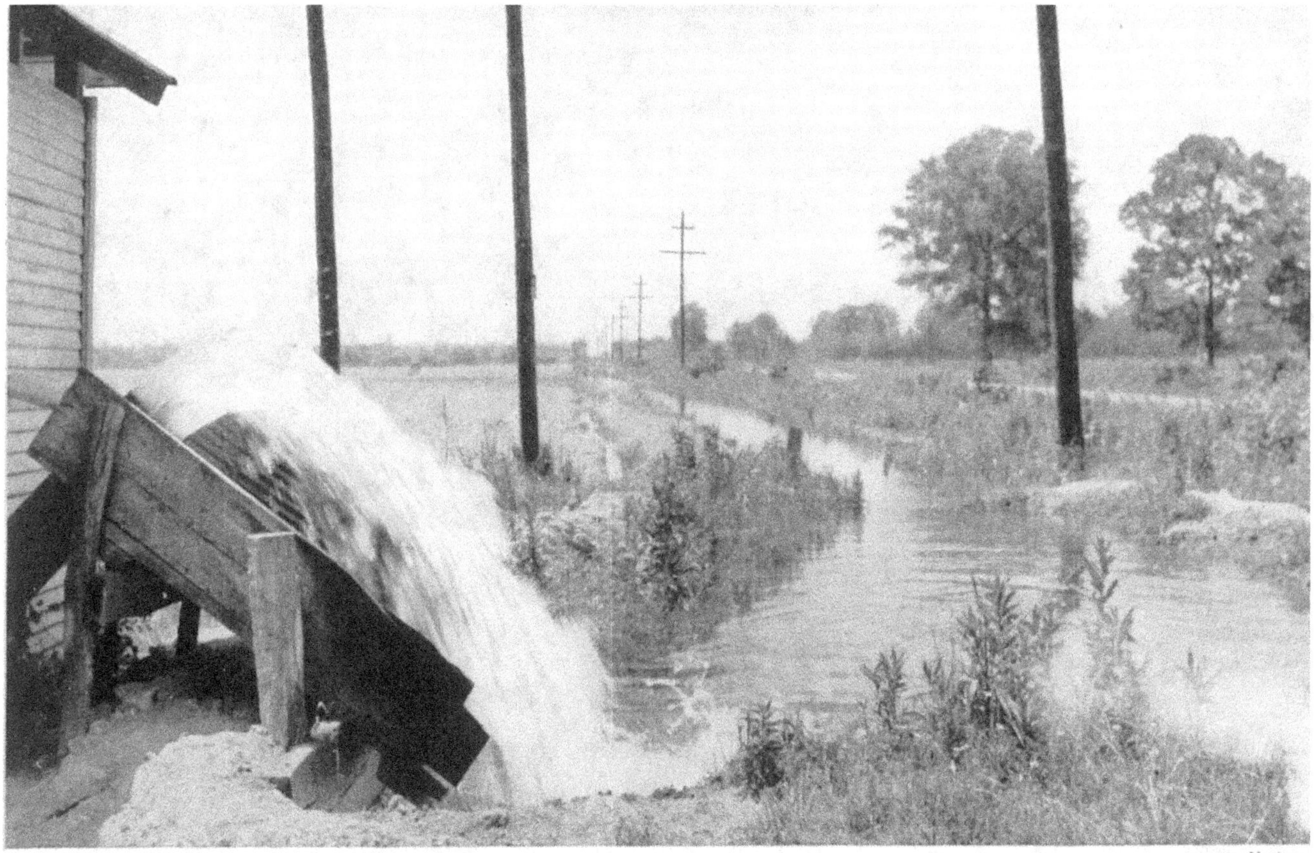

FSA Mydans

An electric pump, the newest type of water pump used in the Arkansas rice fields, near Harrisburg.

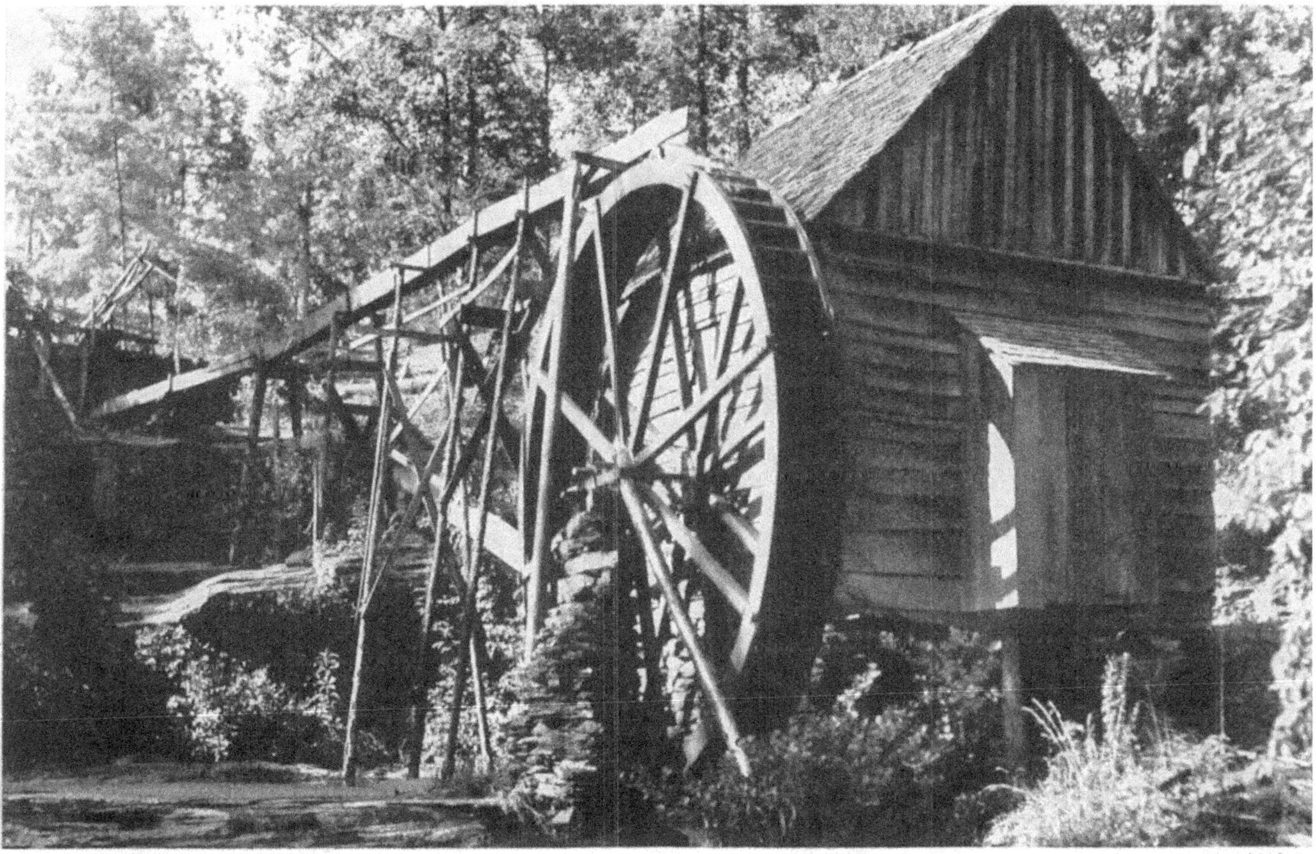

FSA Mydans

The water wheel of an active grist mill three miles from Cornelia, in Northern Georgia.

FSA *Rothstein*
A farm home in Wayne County, North Carolina, made livable by government aid.

FSA *Rothstein*
A resettled family in Johnson County, North Carolina.

FSA *Mydans*
The trading post at Cumberland Homesteads, Crossville, Tennessee.

FSA *Rothstein*
The store at Skyline Farms, Alabama.

FSA *Evans*
A resettlement project near Eatonton, Georgia.

FSA *Mydans*
A five-room house at the Palmerdale Homesteads, Alabama.

"THE TENANT PROBLEM OF THE SOUTH IS A COMMUNITY, REGIONAL, AND NATIONAL QUESTION."

VILLAGES FOR VILLAGERS

ment.* The program should be of a general nature rather than of specific planning. It should include a reconstruction and reorganization of existing communities and not aim entirely at new creations. It should as far as possible utilize local government, local color and local traditions. It should fit in with the community guidance and improvement already being fostered through the agricultural extension service, the land grant colleges, and other agencies. There should be effective provisions and guarantees for the inclusion of Negroes in the village renaissance. There are more than a dozen Negro towns and villages in the South. It is perhaps a fair statement to say that Negroes naturally take more interest than whites in village life, and yet such life for them is more cramped. They furnish good human material for organization and coöperation, just as they have long furnished good material for exploitation.

There should be no thought of applying any Danish or Irish village pattern to the South. No pattern will fit the whole South. The dynamic sections of mechanized farming require a different treatment from those which must have a more intensive manual labor cultivation to survive. The little farmers of the hills have different needs from those of the large farmers of the plains. The strawberry farmers require community organizations which are different from the needs of cotton farmers. But it is well to remember that what farmers have done farmers can do. The experience of Denmark and other countries during the past fifty years shows that farmers can coöperate among themselves and with their government in organizing for better farming and better communities. The South needs the teaching and the application of that experience.

Government budgetary arguments should not be allowed to oppose a public program of village development, for the public liabilities would be accompanied by public assets, both economic and social. The financing would be nationally internal, not foreign, and could be adjusted to any proper period of amortization. If its cost must come out of individual

---

* W. T. Couch, writing in *The American Review* for June, 1934, suggested that the Federal government undertake the establishment of four or five thousand attractive farm villages in the South. Such a program could not be planned rigidly and carried out over night but could be undertaken on a flexible and gradual basis.

incomes sooner or later, it represents a redressing of income distribution in favor of a deficit farm class. It is incidentally easier to maintain decent government, schools and churches in a system of home-owned villages than in a system of widely scattered homesteads and tenant farms. The program would not be a job of charity, but would be a policy of helping people help themselves. It would facilitate a program of more intensive farming, of balanced farming, and of balance between farming and industrial pursuits, including handicrafts. It would permit more people to live and live well in the South. It would permit the South to avoid a population crisis, which seems to be upon us. It would neutralize the opinion of a group of population experts who say the old cotton belt must export more than a million human beings to save itself. Higher village standards of living and culture will reduce the South's high birth rate and relieve the region of the burden of being the human breeding ground of the nation.

CHAPTER EIGHT

LOCAL INDUSTRIES AND WORKSHOPS

VILLAGE AND LOCAL INDUSTRIES HAVE A REAL INFLUENCE ON RURAL SOCIETY and on the status of farmers. It is important to observe the industrial trends of the rural South and give them as healthy a direction as possible. Little sawmills, many of them portable, manufacture a large proportion of the South's lumber output and pay farmers many millions annually for timber. Paper mills are invading Southern timber areas and offering future possibilities. Turpentine industries get raw material in Southern areas of piney woods. Cotton gins, grist mills, feed mills, syrup mills, and canneries are factors in the economy of rural communities. Much of the textile manufacturing, cotton-oil milling, and tobacco processing is carried on in farm-district towns and villages. The hill towns, villages and hamlets of the northwestern corner of Georgia realize several million dollars a year from making and selling tufted bedspreads. Handmade products of different kinds are available to tourists in the Great Smokies. There are village hosiery mills, garment plants and furniture factories. Occasionally a cabinet shop or hooked-rug establishment shows up on a country roadside. Repair plants, especially for automobiles, deserve mention. There are too few creameries.

Available labor and raw materials make Southern towns inviting centers for new industries. Cheap power and efficient highway transportation facilitate the physical decentralization of many types of industries, as a few village leaders have realized. New industrial opportunities confront the South with every wave of prosperity. The Southern press in the past few years has been active in praising its region as an ideal one for new manufacturing. Town governments and state legislatures encourage new industries with official inducements. The state of Louisiana in 1936 ratified a constitutional amendment to grant taxation favors to new industries. The state of Mississippi has taken the lead in officially seeking new business and new manufacturing.

The Mississippi legislature in 1936 passed a law, sponsored by Governor White, "to protect its people by balancing agriculture with industry." It provided for a state industrial commission with power to authorize counties, supervisors' districts, and municipalities to acquire industrial enterprises and issue bonds for them, to operate the industries and dispose of them, and "generally to make such contracts relative to such industries as are essential." Local elections must favor acquisition or establishment of an industry, but this approval is not required for the sale of a plant by the local governing body. New enterprises thus initiated are exempt from all ad valorem taxation for five years. The law fails to make provision for labor relations, conditions and standards, or for the conservation of the state's physical resources. It sets up a regime which tends to shift the burden of property taxes more heavily against farmers, who constitute the most numerous group in Mississippi. It reflects no interest in coöperative enterprise by or for farmers and consumers. It is in accord with a policy, unfortunately too prevalent in Mississippi and neighboring states, of attracting "carpetbaggers of industry" southward from high wage areas with arguments of cheap labor and freedom from social control.

The South needs industrial plants but not tax-exempt establishments which can not pay fair wages and which can not stand alone when the period of exemption is over. Local governments, bankers and laborers have in many cases discovered that bargain plants are of small benefit in the long run and seriously interfere with legitimate manufacturers who are trying to pay decent wages. Occasionally an editor is bold enough to say so, as has George McLean, of the Tupelo (Mississippi) *Journal*. The New York *World-Telegram* and other Scripps-Howard papers, some

Spreading out apples to dry, Nicholson Hollow, Shenandoah National Park.

This storm cellar near Batesville, Arkansas, is also used to store hundreds of cans of food.

Making sorghum syrup, Fuquay Springs, North Carolina.

Pressing sugar cane, Fuquay Springs, North Carolina.

A village grist mill at Nethers, Shenandoah National Park.

Fishing adds to the farm income in Plaquemines Parish, Louisiana

"COMMUNITY ECONOMIC ACTIVITIES WHICH COULD WELL BE ENCOURAGED... IN THE RURAL SOUTH."

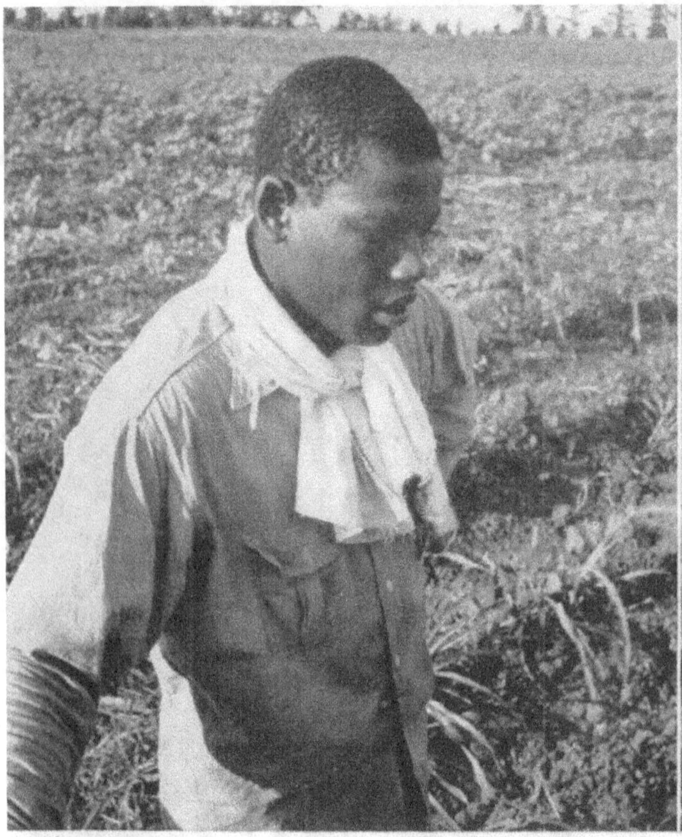

FSA Lange

Cultivating with a hoe, Coahomo County, Mississippi.

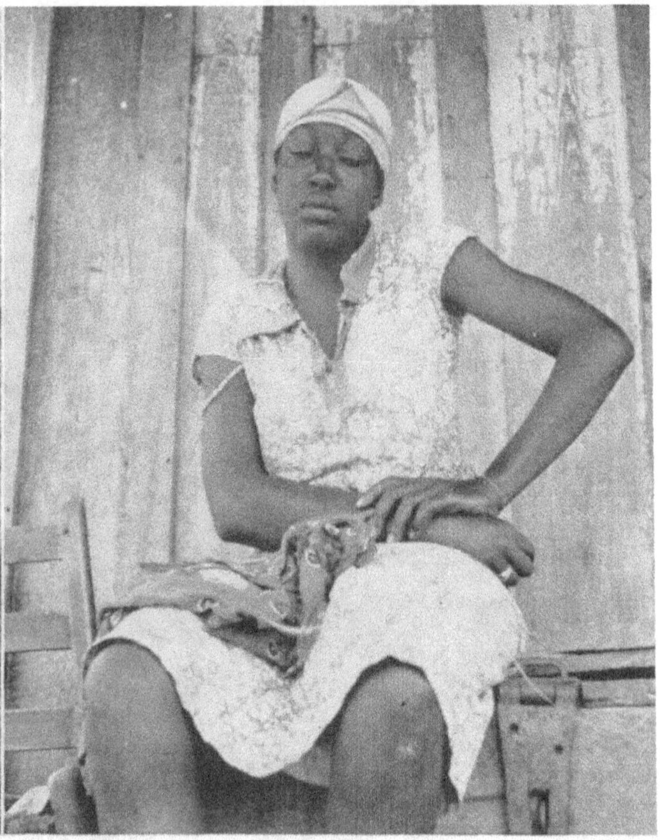

FSA Lange

Just in from the cotton field.

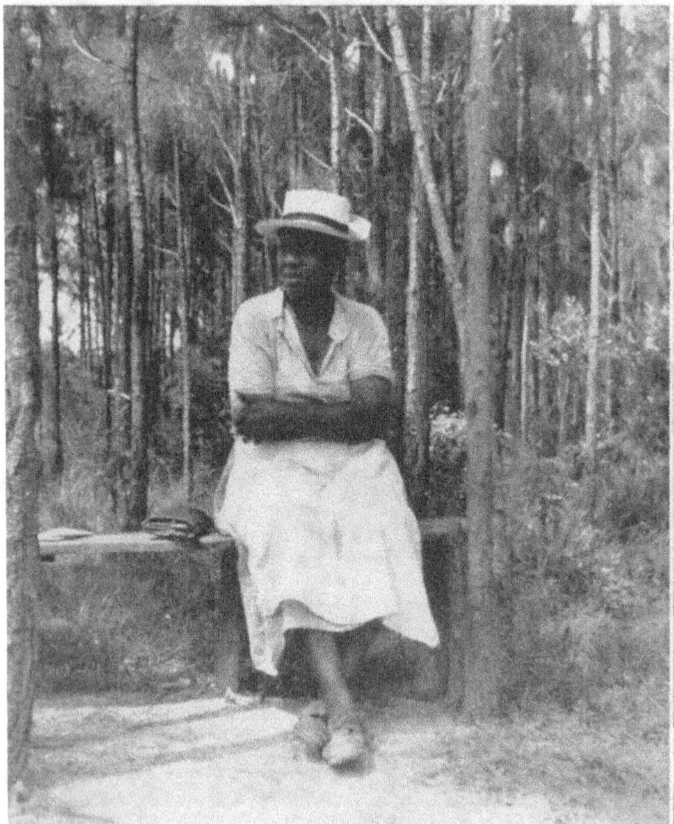

FSA Lange

A land owner in Mississippi.

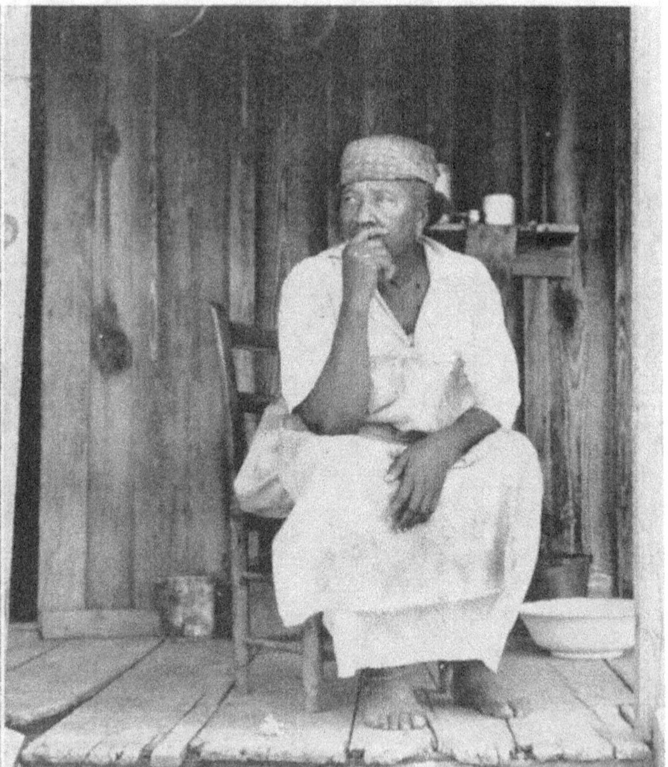

FSA Lange

A share cropper woman in Hinds County, Mississippi.

"IT IS DIFFICULT FOR THE LIGHT OF TUSKEGEE TO PENETRATE SHARE-CROPPER DARKNESS."

LOCAL INDUSTRIES AND WORKSHOPS

months ago, published a series of articles on the trek of industries to favor-granting towns of the South. The articles were written by Thomas L. Stokes, a native of Atlanta, who visited small towns in several states to get actual facts on the labor situation. He found low wages, long hours, dissatisfied labor, and social abuses, including various ways of reducing nominal wages to miserable levels. He found Dickson, Tennessee, disillusioned after experience with a subsidized garment plant which the town had invited, the mayor saying, "I want 'em out." In Georgia he found small towns bidding for concerns situated in Atlanta, where labor unions count for something. He found cases of Southern towns' extending financial aid to garment factories and pledging future deductions from wages, with workers signing for contributions from their meager pay.

The industrial complaints against the importation of cheap goods from Japan and other foreign lands of low wages should also be turned on the Mississippi industrial plan and on the policies of those numerous Southern towns which extend taxation privileges as well as poor labor standards to new industries. The state of Mississippi, where lumber companies have dominated local governing bodies, should expand its slender labor legislation before inviting outsiders to come in and exploit its human and physical resources. The Mississippi plan and other methods of industrial favoritism only sink the South deeper into a colonial economy and increase the extra-regional control of the South by private business. There are examples of Northern manufacturers who have moved to the South, who have paid less than they took away, and who have only served as agents for collecting tribute. Subsidizing sub-marginal manufacturers of cheap goods is a poor way to improve an agricultural commonwealth. However, the economic conditions which permit sweat-factories to enter a community cry out for remedy. The South often has labor to spare. The South seems to be always in need of industries.

Balancing agriculture with industry in any absolute or approximate sense may not be proper for a Southern state like Mississippi any more than balancing industry with agriculture would be wise for an industrial district like Birmingham or Pittsburgh or Detroit. Mississippi and similar agricultural states might well adopt a moderate and evolutionary program of industrialization. Before rushing too much into a policy of balancing agriculture with industry, they could, with wisdom and benefit, give more attention to balancing their agriculture. Most or all of the old cotton states could produce more livestock for food and eat it, more milk and drink it, more hay, peas or grain and feed it, without affecting anybody's market. They could increase these products for home consumption without reducing the amount of cotton and other crops produced for cash, though the annual acreage of cash crops would be less. Increased productivity as well as economic independence for Mississippi's farmers can be brought about without artificial attempts to establish state industrial autonomy.

There are community economic activities which could well be encouraged and even subsidized by state or local governments and civic groups in the rural South. Aid and education in the coöperative canning of fruits and vegetables for small farmers would improve the winter diet of rural families as well as the marketing of these products. Better facilities for the manufacture of syrup are much needed. The strawberry farmers of Louisiana could avoid rushing their crops to a glutted market if they had the use of community refrigeration or cold-packing. Especially is it true that up-country sorghum syrup is frequently of poor quality because of faulty methods of milling and cooking. I have known hillbillies to quit growing sorghum cane because they could not count on its being converted into good syrup at the right time.* Feed-mills for chopping and mixing home-grown products are too scarce and "far-between." Many a community could use a coöperative sawmill, which should not be operated for profit and destruction but for a gradual use of timber on a basis of conservation and local needs. Coöperative cotton ginning offers benefits to groups of yeomen farmers and makes it possible for them to realize much more for cotton seed through larger sales and contracts. Federal credit is available for such farmer undertakings. The Bank for Coöperatives at New Orleans during the first half of 1937 completed the

* It is encouraging to note the interest of members of the TVA staff in perfecting and standardizing scientific methods of cooking sorghum and getting them applied.

LOCAL INDUSTRIES AND WORKSHOPS

financing for five coöperative cotton gins. Reductions of farm tenancy would permit an expansion of this activity. Farmer coöperation in the mixing of fertilizer, which has been successfully tried, should meet the needs of local soils more adequately than distant products of standardized analyses. The increased planting of soil-improvement crops emphasizes fertilizer selectivity and the omission of costly ingredients. Any kind or degree of fertilizer economy for farmers is earnestly to be wished.

There are various needs as well as opportunities for improved processing of Southern farm products for home use and for market. More of this processing would call for farm village activity and employment. Other coöperative activities might include local breeding associations, for instance, to displace razor-back hogs and those milch cows which are expensive boarders. There is urgent need for public or coöperative facilities for small farm terracing under the national program of soil conservation. A hill county official recently gave me the story of a county board's experiment with purchasing terracing machinery and terracing lands for farmers who paid for the cost of operation. The county government got full pay again in the reduced upkeep of country roads through less flooding from rains.

The depression brought a revival of handicrafts in many regions. Relief authorities and other government agencies have utilized this method of furnishing employment. Every farm village should have a work center in which young people might make or learn to make articles for use, beauty or sale. There is something to the claim as to the superiority of the use of tools over the use of machines in the development of personality. Skills in the use of tools, combined with an expansion of home ownership, would bring many physical improvements to dwellings and other properties. The Berry school in North Georgia, Berea in Kentucky, and other institutions, have shown what can be done in the development of handicrafts among mountain boys and girls. The artistic possibilities of handicrafts are sponsored by some thirty federated groups and schools in the Southern mountain region. Handicrafts for Negro youth constitute part of the achievements of Tuskegee Institute. Such work and training should be made available to the youth of both races without its being necessary for them to go off to school or to get in the bread-line before having the opportunity. Southern farm regions have a shortage of skilled workers in comparison with common laborers, and Southern villages are not free from the physical signs of a shortage of good craftsmanship.

Village workshops could be used to reduce idleness and delinquency. It should be the purpose to give the work centers an atmosphere of recreation and to operate them for the benefit of the workers, preferably on a coöperative basis. Rigid precautions should prevent them from becoming disguised sweat-shops, as was seemingly true of a few Mississippi WPA projects for "industrial training schools," which were reported to have been canceled by order of Harry Hopkins.

The bedspread industry is furnishing part-time employment to some thousands of Georgia farm families but on a sweated labor basis. This is true whether the hand labor is performed at home or in town work "houses." There are authentic cases of women working for less than two dollars per week in the interim of prosperity. They need organization, coöperation, and official protection in the interest of the general welfare. The profit system should not be allowed to force women and children to slave for a mere pittance to supplement receipts from hill cotton crops. It should be possible to turn this bedspread industry into a decent system of supplementing agricultural employment and income. The beautiful spreads "on the line" in front of the rural homes are in too striking contrast with the general surroundings and appearance of the houses of the workers.

It is important for Southern towns and villages to appreciate the connection between high wages and high productivity as well as purchasing power. Low wages and low productivity tend to go together. The South can not prosper with labor that borders on peonage, which has existed in certain lumber camps. It is to be hoped that the paper industry, which is moving into Southern woods, and the possible newsprint development will not exploit rural village labor as well as our timber resources. Collective bargaining may henceforth be relied upon for the protection of labor interests in large urban and interstate industries. But many local in-

LOCAL INDUSTRIES AND WORKSHOPS

dustries in farm communities of the South will not be directly affected by labor organizations for many years. The public conscience and the public power must safeguard our village labor against demoralization. Village merchants might see more clearly that retail sales vary directly with wages and employment. They should apply the point of this relationship to the protection of Negro labor against semi-starvation wages. Negro laborers are good spenders. A colored worker once gave me his pay-day philosophy by saying, "The eagle on the dollar means to let 'er fly and I lets 'er fly."

The South is in a position to avoid some of the worst social evils of the industrial revolution which England experienced in the last of the eighteenth and first part of the nineteenth century, and which New England experienced a little later. The evils are known, and many of them have been dealt with by the more sophisticated industrial regions. We should not repeat the recognized mistakes, and Southern towns should not rush into industrialization with all rules and standards down. The town welcome-sign to new plants should carry a speed limit, a limit on the production of cheap goods with cheap labor. The South indeed needs a certain amount of outside capital for the development of its resources, but control of the affairs of Southern towns should not be surrendered to absentee owners of industries, for the absentee control of towns for private gain may be as baneful as the absentee control of farms. Absentee control frequently stands in the way of fair labor relations. Cut-throat competition among towns for industries does not pay and should be prevented. It is difficult, but nevertheless wise, for towns to avoid attempts to become large or rich quickly. A newspaper man of a county-seat town a year or two ago was talking to me and lamenting the town's lack of industrial growth. He said it was on the industrial blacklist for being too much in the grip of organized labor. I asked him about his paper's circulation and he answered, "An all time high." Incidentally this town, with diversified industries and farm support, escaped bank troubles in the late depression. It should praise the policy which has seemingly been saddled upon it. Southern town leaders might well give attention to an increase in quality production, to higher types of processing, for Southern industrial products generally represent low values added by manufacturing. Exclusive low-stage processing is characteristic of a colonial economy and of economic dependence. This principle applies equally to the processing of agricultural products. The status of many a forty-acre or hundred-acre farmer in the South could be elevated by improved facilities for packing, processing, or storing his products, whether cotton or hay, fruit or vegetables, eggs or milk. The South does not consume enough milk, and yet milk sometimes goes to waste on small farms for the lack of facilities for handling and marketing it.

Every farm village or farm market town owes it to itself and its community to sponsor the development of physical facilities and farmer coöperation for the better preservation and processing of agricultural products. Particularly should all possible steps be taken to make cheap electric power available to villagers and farmers. Electricity is needed on the farm for various mechanical and refrigeration purposes as well as for lighting the premises. It can saw wood, pump water, thrash peas, preserve eggs and butter, or furnish light to read agricultural bulletins.

It is essential that there be coöperation within the town as well as between town and country in order to bring on a rural renaissance. Short-term profits for a few individuals must be sacrificed for a general increase in the production, income and welfare of the community. But community coöperation is not enough. There must be a degree of coöperation and common action among all the communities of a region. No community can stand alone in the machine age. It is as important for villages as for individuals that they be integrated under a system of social control for their own good, that they be protected against themselves and against an external acquisitive pressure. The scattered government community experiments and the local coöperative ventures are esoteric and can have no wide effect on rural life unless fitted into a regional or national picture. Village planning should be coördinated with a more general regional planning and action.

"THE SOUTH IS IN URGENT NEED OF SCIENTIFIC FORESTRY."

Planting slash pine, Macon County, Alabama.

FSA *Rothstein*

A good stand of shortleaf pine, fifteen to twenty years old, near Farmville, Virginia.

FSA *Carter*

Pulpwood going down the River Styx to Mobile, Alabama.

FSA *Lange*

"THE DEPLETION OF THE SOIL, WHICH SOUTHERNERS LOVE SO MUCH AND ABUSE SO MUCH."

Through repeated crops of cotton, the soil of this Alabama farm has been "sold in annual installments."

FSA *Rothstein*

Cotton was grown on this field twenty-five years ago.

FSA *Rothstein*

The effects of tenancy and constant cropping on a hillside field.

FSA *Rothstein*

CHAPTER NINE

SOCIAL PLANNING AND ACTION

THE SOUTH MUST PLAN FOR SOCIAL ACTION OR RESIGN ITSELF TO POVERTY and disintegration.* There is no escape from such a choice through industrial or agricultural individualism. The South has been a heavy exporter of physical and human resources with little regard to the conservation of these resources. Its forests have been cut and sold and not replanted. Its coal and iron have been mined to make steel for the enrichment of absentees. The substance of its soil has been taken away through exhaustive crops faster than it was replaced, and much of the land has been washed into the sea. The land robbery has, in effect, robbed the

* The extensive and organized research which culminated in H. W. Odum's *Southern Regions* (Chapel Hill, 1936) shows that there are important unutilized resources in the South, that our actuality of achievement lags far behind our potentiality. The lag between actuality and potentiality seems greater in the South than in any other similarly populous area of the United States. Much more research on the Southern areas is needed for the guidance of social planning and the determination of intelligent action. But it is futile to await all the research returns before attempting a few major lines of planning and action. Besides *Southern Regions*, we have additional studies by Odum, Rupert Vance, Thomas J. Woofter, Jr., Charles S. Johnson, Wilson Gee, the late E. C. Branson, and others. The National Resources Committee, the TVA, and WPA, the Farm Security Administration, the President's Committee on Farm Tenancy, and other Federal government agencies have discovered and presented an abundance of social data on the South. There are studies by state and university authorities and by independent groups, such as the Southern Policy Committee. There is, in other words, a rather formidable array of data and interpretation available for use. Planning is trailing research somewhat afar, though Southern state planning agencies are in existence.

people of the soil of productive power through lack of income, health and education.

The South has an unbalanced budget.* It has deficit areas or units of government and people, which nevertheless contribute something to the wealth and welfare of others. Grainger County, Tennessee, is an example which might be repeated. The economic status of that county, which is partly flooded by the water above Norris Dam, has been analyzed in a TVA study.** It is a mountain agricultural county. In 1932 its income from the rest of the world was $465,000, exclusive of state and Federal aid and insurance, in comparison with $820,000, estimated for outgo, depreciation and soil depletion. The outgo included $85,000 of interest and $20,000 of outside tax payments. The deficit was only partially offset by state aid for schools and roads of $60,000, Federal aid of $51,000, and net insurance receipts of $32,000. It is correct to say that the inhabitants of Grainger and similarly situated counties have a poor opportunity to earn a living. It seems fair also to say that by any test of justice they do not get all they earn. Revision of their earning and purchasing power would be good statesmanship and good business. If the TVA can do anything to protect or remove Grainger from an economy of the Dark Ages, then the manufacturers' associations should thank the TVA.

The Tennessee Valley Authority is a government-owned corporation endowed with the three functions of research, planning, and action in a region where population growth has been exerting a heavy pressure on the prevailing economy. It is concerned directly with navigation improvement, flood control, soil conservation, and hydro-electric development, not to mention potential national defense. All these factors vitally affect agricultural, industrial, and social trends, in which the Authority is incidentally but exceedingly interested.

The TVA can neither make nor execute a blue print for a new system of communities or civilization. Its role of agricultural and industrial

---

* See D. C. Coyle, "The South's Unbalanced Budget," *The Virginia Quarterly Review*, XIII (Spring, 1937), 192-208.

** This study is summarized by Stuart Chase in an article, "TVA: The New Deal's Greatest Asset," in *The Nation*, CXLII (June 3, 1936), 702-705.

planning must be limited by national and constitutional considerations. It carries on education and demonstration for better farming and better living, coöperating with local and state governments as well as with various agricultural agencies. Its efforts are avowedly directed toward raising the economic level of an entire region, rather than alleviating specific cases of dependency. Its objectives are long-range, not immediate. Its program for improvement of forestry, soils and crops will require time to reveal full regional benefits, and in the meantime the whole project will not fill as large a place as many expect. The emphasis on rural electrification is significant for a region in which there has been so little rural use of electricity. Promoting low-cost electricity and electrical appliances is a distinctly effective influence for higher standards of production and of living. Significant also is the policy of the Authority in selling surplus electric power, of giving preference to counties, municipalities, and coöperative organizations of citizens and farmers. There are examples of small groups of farmers maintaining walk-in refrigerators under TVA encouragement, with dietary and economic gains. It is a distinct boon to make refrigeration available to country stores. There are advantages to Southern rural communities served by private power companies, which have generally adopted sympathetic policies of rural service since the TVA came into activity.

The TVA is an organized attempt to plan for plenty and to escape scarcity. It may be fairly called the strongest card in the New Deal. It is the greatest movement in the South for modernizing agriculture, conserving rural manhood, and facilitating village development. It should prove a godsend to hillbillies. It represents extra-regional capital and a measure of extra-regional control, but from Washington, not from Wall Street. The deficit South needs this outside capital, and the inarticulate underprivileged of the region should not object to a little democratic control from the outside. It is sincerely to be hoped that local capital as well as local planning will come more and more into play in coördination with the national effort. The nation needs a series of grand projects of the TVA type, as President Roosevelt has proposed, but it seems fortunate that the eroded South became the scene of the first experiment.

FORTY ACRES AND STEEL MULES

The control of cotton production since 1933 can be pointed to as about the most effective regional planning which has occurred in the cotton belt. The effectiveness of this program resulted from government participation and from acceptance by Southern landlords. Much of the credit for the program is due to the Farm Bureau Federations and other organizations of Southern states. The program has been improved along the way and has contributed to a more scientific land-crop policy. Southerners can not praise too highly its soil-improvement features. It has demonstrated the practical efficacy of regional coöperation and planning in a national setting. The propertyless and disfranchised farmers have not had adequate protection in the making and execution of the program, but be it said that these farmers have seldom or never had adequate protection. The program has failed to emphasize effectively the growing of cotton in sub-regions where that commodity can be produced cheaply or efficiently and to discourage cotton growing in sub-regions of inefficiency. More attention should be given to aiding certain areas to grow more cotton and aiding other areas to grow less cotton. The sections of hills, small fields and patches should be encouraged or subsidized not to attempt competition with the sections where steel mules and other farm machinery are on the increase and where the cotton-picker may soon be speeding along the cotton rows. This intra-regional adjustment is one of the large problems among the many pressing problems of the cotton economy.

Public policy with respect to land and crops in the South or for the South should take account of the large proportion of corporation holdings and corporation farming, especially in the communities where the land is most productive. It is important to recognize that the corporate plantation involves a wage-labor problem, often distinct from tenancy and small-farmer coöperation. This is widely true in the operation of sugar plantations. Rural labor relations can not justly be left to a laissez-faire solution, while agricultural interests in general are receiving favorable governmental intervention. The moderate regulation of corporation farming, encouragement of coöperative farming, and security for the actual tillers of the soil are essential to a good rural society and are vital

FSA *Rothstein*
A migrant camp on the outskirts of Birmingham.

FSA *Rothstein*
Children of a migrant fruit worker camped near Winter Park, Florida.

FSA *Lange*
Oklahoma migrants living in a house that junk built.

FSA *Rothstein*
Setting out rows of celery, Sanford, Florida.

FSA *Rothstein*
Negro bean pickers hitchhiking, Florida.

FSA *Lange*
Cotton workers carried by truck from Memphis to the plantations in Arkansas.

"THERE IS NO ESCAPE FROM UNEVENNESS OF EMPLOYMENT AMONG SOUTHERN FARM WORKERS."

"The town welcome sign to new plants should carry a speed limit, a limit on the production of cheap goods with cheap labor.... The South needs industrial plants, but not tax-exempt establishments."

An effective community center can not develop in an inadequately housed and supported Negro school.

Public library in the piney woods of southern Mississippi. "It is important that a wider reading public be developed..."

Note the dark, unfinished windowless interior of this rural school in Arkansas. "Modern school expansion is circumscribed by the South's limited school revenues and by the splitting of school funds as well as systems between the two races."

SOCIAL PLANNING AND ACTION

as matters of state. Consideration of these essentials should enter into land, crop and tax programs.

The Farm Security Administration and other Federal authorities have been concerned with removing farmers and "squatters" from submarginal lands to areas where cultivation of the soil will yield a living. The President's farm tenancy committee had much to say on this point. But during the depression, the movement to poor lands was infinitely greater than the subsidized transfer of families from such areas. State action seems absolutely necessary to prevent this back-to-poor-land movement, especially by farmers in hard times. It might as well be admitted that the South has stretches of lands which, from the point of view of intensive agriculture, are suitable only "to hold the world together." The products of portions of such lands can properly nourish neither man nor beast. Investigations of chemists and agriculturists indicate that certain Southern soils are deficient in calcium and other body building minerals. Their experiments show that pigs and chickens fed continually from the grain produced on these calcium-deficient soils develop bone weaknesses, crooked legs, and knotty knees, with signs of poor muscular development.* Since these areas are generally given over to subsistence types of farming, the human population is liable to suffer from the same deficiencies. It would seem wise to turn such areas over to timber, wild life, and recreation.

The farmers of the Southeast particularly should be encouraged, educated and directed toward a greater production of livestock and non-cotton crops, a more scientific use of suitable lands, and an avoidance of poor lands for intensive cropping. Such a planned policy will coördinate with an expansion of cotton production in the Southwest and with a greater emphasis on forestry and forestry products in the Southeast.

The South, with its heavy loss from erosion and its excessive fertilizer bill, should be the leading section to apply as fully as possible the national program, recommendations, and aid for the improvement of land use

---

* Professor O. D. Duncan, of Oklahoma Agricultural and Mechanical College, has collected information and expert opinion on this phase of the relationship between poor man and poor land.

and land policy. The states of this region should adopt strong legislation and measures for search and support of a program of rural planning in harmony with major trends. The planning should embrace private lands as well as public holdings, for all land use is a matter of public interest and concern. Farmers should not be permitted to ruin hillside forests and then to ruin the soil of the hills by repeated crops of cotton. The community has the right and duty to intervene to save its hills from such destruction. Urban and suburban zoning has been in existence for many years. It is time to give attention to rural zoning with reference to agriculture. Southern states might with profit study the Wisconsin rural zoning system and its results. Under a legislative enabling act of 1929, Wisconsin counties may adopt regulations for zoning lands for agriculture, forestry, and recreation. More than one fourth of the counties of the state have established zoning systems. Many Southern counties need something similar to this system.

The South is in urgent need of planning for scientific forestry, which incidentally offers handsome returns in both cash and conservation. Timber grows rapidly in this region and furnishes an economic supplement to agriculture. Southern farm woods have yielded a revenue ranging close to $100,000,000 per annum. The South can lead the country in systematic forestry development. In the piney woods, grazing, pulp wood, and naval stores can be combined for revenue along with timber growing. It is an incidentally hopeful sign to see more and better livestock along roadsides in Southern woods, though "cattle at large" may interfere with automobile driving. But timber conservation policies need more impetus. Many of the larger lumber and timber companies have adopted policies of conservation, cultivation and gradual use of trees in place of the older method of speedily cutting all the supply and moving to other areas to exploit. Necessity dictates that they switch from old wasteful methods. But the operators of portable mills frequently have little hesitancy in stripping woodlands of every tree which can be run through a sawmill. The advent of the small mill has been the chief cause of over-cutting in the South in recent years. Forestry Service investigations show that in many cases farmers, including owners of mills, have sacrificed stumpage

SOCIAL PLANNING AND ACTION

for immediate cash income, though selective cutting and careful milling would have yielded an equal income without the sacrifice of adequate growing stock. Much can be done for the protection and the orderly development of Southern farm woodlands. It is particularly important to husband this resource properly, with paper mills coming south. These mills take smaller-size timber and can exploit more rapidly than can sawmills. The South stands first in the nation as a source of cordwood-size timber suited to pulp and paper manufacture. Much of this potential supply is on farms. Federal, state and landowner coöperation should be utilized to the fullest extent for the maximum development of these farm woods. The owners have been the most backward in such coöperation, not making use of the available state and Federal services. More than education is needed. Farmers have been brought into short-term crop programs. It is time to adopt effective measures to bring them into long-term forestry programs.

Planning agencies should give careful attention to the possibilities of putting chemistry to work for Southern farmers, as is indicated by the Farm Chemurgic Council, which represents a recent promotional movement. Cotton-oil products are among the gains from the connection between applied science and agriculture, and a recent eulogy calls cotton seed gray diamonds. Not content to stop with the cotton lint and seed, experts are experimenting with cotton stalks for new products. There are possibilities for the South in soy beans and in processing them into various industrial products which Henry Ford and others consume in further production. Tung oil offers commensurate returns for cheap lands. George Washington Carver, of Tuskegee, has derived numerous delicacies from the South's lowly peanut. Starch from sweet potatoes seems a successful undertaking at Laurel, Mississippi. An excellent synthetic board is made from bagasse, the refuse of sugar cane after the juice has been expressed. The illustrations might be continued. Research for new uses is being carried on regularly at the agricultural colleges. Chemistry and improved processing can create new sources of income for Southern farmers, and these new sources of income should be provided. But in these developments farmers should be protected by expert advice

FORTY ACRES AND STEEL MULES

and by organizations of their own against mistakes and exploitation. Planning boards and agricultural authorities should endeavor to safeguard the interests of all farmers with respect to these scientific trends. Over-prediction of results should be guarded against, and growers of unprotected staples should not be lured by industrial chemists' propaganda into an advocacy of high tariff doctrines. Chemurgy seems to be a tall tale on a nationalistic scale. The preachers of the blessings of chemistry might give more consideration to the agricultural South's need for cheaper commercial fertilizer, which is partly bolstered up in price by tariff barriers.

The Southern states need the benefits of a maximum coöperation with the Federal government in the Social Security program. The inadequacies of the program especially affect this section. Farm laborers, share croppers, and domestic servants are left out of the unemployment insurance provisions of the system, and, in the South, these three classes together constitute a group of several hundred thousand workers, whose earnings are too low for any guarantee of individual security. They constitute a major problem, which is not to be obscured by seasonal or prosperous periods of good employment. Something can be done through town and rural slum clearance to provide them more adequate shelter. But landed security for most farm laborers and croppers seems out of the question for years and years. An expansion among rural workers of the labor union movement will furnish farm laborers protection against certain abuses, but this will hardly touch the major problem of insecurity. There is no escape from unevenness of employment among Southern farm workers in view of agricultural changes, mechanization, market fluctuations, and seasonal variations. No payroll tax system for workers' security can be applied to farmers as a class. More adequate social security for farm workers might be supported by income and corporation taxes. The failure of the national plan to provide security as to agricultural unemployment relatively increases the burden of providing for dependent children in rural districts, for farm workers have many children. This gap in the system is a serious matter for the South and its great flock of rural children.

Medical planning is an urgent need of the rural South with its high

SOCIAL PLANNING AND ACTION

birth rate and scarcity of physicians. The orthodox health board services have improved throughout the region, and health studies by authorities subsidized by endowed foundations have increased disease control. Aid to crippled children and to rural health work is provided in the national Social Security Act. But physicians have been running away from rural villages and towns of the South. Medical service is difficult for families who are dependent upon charity. The large number of farm families just above the charity line can not afford a case of illness. A pay case for operation and hospitalization frequently means loss of farm and home. A former agricultural college dean and practical farmer has observed the direct and indirect effects of medical cost on the status of farm families, and he has found this cause an important one in preventing or wrecking farm ownership. His observation can be confirmed. I have known farmers to go "broke" on account of doctor bills. I have known members of rural families to leave hospitals several days too soon after operations, for the reason that they could not afford the cost of more time in the hospital. It is true that small-town physicians perform many services for charity. But several years of experience with a rural telephone toll station taught me that some doctors hesitate to answer a night call from poor country people, if there is no word from a respectable guarantor. This hesitancy seemed to increase with the passing of horse-and-buggy doctors. Yet the present-day ruralites, removed from pioneer hardiness and pioneer home remedies, require greater professional service than did their ancestors.

Socialized or public medical service is the only effective answer to the serious shortage of physicians in the rural Southeast, where the human demand for service is great and the per capita ability to pay is low. The medical profession, on an individualistic basis, can not adequately correct the shortage and can not save unfortunate families from the burden of heavy medical costs. The economic demand must be moved up to equate with the human demand, and the cost must be so distributed as not to fall too heavily upon any member of society. If medical aid to charity patients in the country can be systemized and subsidized, facilities for group medical service will serve the purpose of farm families who are able to pay. Coöperation for better medical attention will mean as much to farmers as any coöperative activity they may undertake. Public action to encourage such a movement is in order, and it should be mentioned that several group or coöperative undertakings for medical service are sponsored by the Farm Security Administration. There is equal need for group hospitalization for farm families or hospital service at rates which persons with small incomes can pay, even if taxes must be collected to make this possible. The feeling of insecurity as to health causes not a few wage-earners and farm tenants, including many Negroes, to feed premiums at short intervals into sickness and accident insurance systems, which only imperfectly meet their needs. This practice seems to illustrate both the condition and the opportunity which call for socialized medicine.

There must be a planning for democratic education beyond the school room and the school year, if social action is to be effective, intelligent and democratic. It is important that technical knowledge be humanized and publicized among the masses, that the extension services of the land-grant colleges be spread more widely among tenants and small farmers, and that hillbilly suspicions of planter control of these services be allayed. In spite of the urgency of the Southern farm tenant problem, I could not hear a word about it at the "farmers' week" conference of a Gulf state agricultural college a summer or two ago. In an executive conference on tenancy in another state, the director of the agricultural extension service sounded a reactionary note, assuming that farm tenants are in a class apart and that little could or should be done about their plight. The extension services must become more than agricultural aids to landlords. The human labor factor is a larger factor in agricultural and industrial production in the South than elsewhere in the United States. Too much attention can not be given to that factor. The state agricultural colleges must dare to build for a new social order as well as for a new order of pigs, cows, and crops.

It is important that a wider reading public be developed in the South and that something to read be provided. The percentage of the population in the region without public library service ranges from fifty-five in North Carolina to eighty-five in Arkansas. More than eighty per cent

FSA *Rothstein*
Flood waters of the Shenandoah River covering a Virginia farm.

FSA *Evans*
The Bessie Levee, along a subsidiary of the Mississippi, near Tiptonville, Tennessee, during the 1937 flood.

FSA *Evans*
The white bread line in the camp at Forrest City, Arkansas.

FSA *Evans*
A line-up for food in the camp for flood refugees, Forrest City, Arkansas.

FSA *Locke*
Demolished by the flood of 1937, Smithland, Kentucky.

FSA *Lange*
A flood refugee family which has wandered from Arkansas to Texas.

THE SOUTH, AT THE RECEIVING END OF VAST DRAINAGE SYSTEMS, IS IN URGENT NEED OF FLOOD CONTROL.

FSA *Rothstein*
On a farm in Cimarron County, Oklahoma.

FSA *Rothstein*
Tumbleweed rolls over submerged machinery after a dust storm.

FSA *Lange*
Oklahoma farmers line the shady side of Main Street while their crops burn up in the drought.

FSA *Rothstein*
Fighting a devastating drought with a thin stream of water.

"DROUGHT CONDITIONS INTENSIFY THE NEED OF RURAL REHABILITATION."

SOCIAL PLANNING AND ACTION

of the South's Negroes have no access to public library facilities. The Julius Rosenwald Fund, the American Library Association, and the TVA have been active and instrumental in extending library service in the Southern region. The state library extension movements in the South might be given more encouragement. It is unfortunate that only three states, North Carolina, Louisiana, and Texas, are maintaining library field work of an amount that is bringing state-wide results. Strong and well financed extension agencies to carry educational service to the people, the whole people, are fundamental needs of the South.

CHAPTER TEN

THE SOUTH'S ROLE IN THE NATION

REGIONAL AND INTRA-REGIONAL PLANNING IS ESSENTIAL IF THE SOUTH is to correct its unbalanced social budget, reduce its poverty, and reach a respectable level of economic security for all. But there must be more than internal planning and action. The reconstruction should be accomplished through democratic leadership and democratic participation, with a broader suffrage for underdog protection. The planning should be coördinated with a constructive policy, and policy implies a role in the nation and in the world. Cotton, for instance, is the economic basis for the most distinctive regional characteristic of the South, but cotton is a world problem and can not be disposed of, either as a subject or a commodity, behind a Southern Chinese-Wall. It would seem foolish to think of dethroning King Cotton, though he should be stripped of absolutism and made a constitutional monarch with a diversified kingdom and a social bill of rights in favor of farmer-labor subjects. The South is still the leading cotton farming region of the world, and cotton, as Peter Molyneaux says, "constitutes more than half the world's annual consumption of fibers of all kinds, including wool, silk, flax, rayon, and the rest." The South must be regional, national, and international with reference to cotton and many other things. Neither regional planning nor community planning is enough to give farmers or farm villages a just place in the economic picture.

It is regionally important that cotton be produced efficiently and scientifically on suitable lands, with plenty of emphasis on soil conservation, and that cotton growing be reduced on poor and unsuitable lands. Such a formula would reduce the hilly acreage of the Southeast, though it would not end cotton production in that sub-region. It could serve only as one plank in a platform of progress. In the national economy the farmers should get more for their cotton in exchange for other commodities, and this fairness of exchange can partly be brought about through moving more cotton into international trade. Changes in cotton exports have meant serious changes in income for many farm families in Texas and in Mississippi. The South should be internationally minded.

It may be said that Southern farmers need protection against the protective tariff system, which cuts into their real income two ways, by reducing the export market for cotton and by holding up the price of various items which they buy. High tariffs were a direct contributing cause of the Civil War, and they have played a vital part in keeping Southern farmers poor, in making possible the conditions portrayed in *Tobacco Road*. The tariff system has become a more important factor since the World War, with the United States, now an industrial creditor nation, trying to export cotton to industrial debtor nations in competition with cotton producing countries which are non-industrial debtor nations. Under such conditions, other nations could not easily buy cotton from us when the United States quit lending them money to pay for our exports. They turned to other sources of supply, to countries like Brazil, whose cotton they could pay for. Because of national and international policies, foreign industrial countries were reducing their annual consumption of Southern cotton more than a million bales by the middle of the Hoover administration and increasing by that amount their consumption of non-American cotton. The crop control program was the Roosevelt administration's answer, with benefit payments to the farmers as offsets to the tariff.

The planning of this cotton program, whatever its advantages to Southern farmers, had to be adjusted to the national scene and had to be accompanied by plans designed to benefit large groups of producers of other agricultural commodities all over the country. The cotton plan had to be dovetailed with the plans for wheat, corn, and hogs, and all the plans had to be worked out in the light of the effects of the American tariff system. One policy of scarcity seemed to call for another policy of scarcity. Both policies have had support as well as opposition from the South, the West, and the East. It is emphatically true that the South is divided, as is the rest of the nation, on the protective tariff issue. Some of the most ardent protectionists are Southern industrialists and sugar planters. Neither the tariff policy nor the crop control policy can be set off and given a regional label. Each might be classed as a national bundle of regional and local issues, on which opinion is divided in Main Street and Wall Street.

Freight-rate discrimination against the South is uppermost in the minds of many industrial champions. Southern governors and TVA spokesmen are giving attention to this problem as a regional issue. Territorial differences in rate structures are recognized facts, and the South can not reach an industrial parity in the face of freight-rate barriers, which tend to keep industrial processing and industrial wages at low stages. But freight discrimination hurts the South because this region must exchange goods with other regions. The same is true of the West, which has had transportation problems and bitter contests over them. The South, as well as the West, can best meet the rate question as a national problem. Is American industrialization to be diffused or to remain geographically concentrated in the area between the Mississippi and the Atlantic and north of the Ohio and Potomac? If industry is to be sprinkled over the agricultural sections and if a more vigorous industrial life is to prevail in our towns and villages, there must be a national unification of rate making with those ends in view. The most enlightened freight-rate policy for the South is one of coöperation with other agricultural sections for the purpose of seeking a national policy for the good of all sections and all classes, including Southern workers. The South can not win on any narrower basis. Only a more wholesome and democratic economy for the nation can bring an end to the colonial economy which hovers over the South.

There is no escape from an inter-regional dependency except through a return to a primitive self-sufficiency and inefficiency, with greater scarcity than our modernized large population could stand. The South can not save itself by attempting to become a self-contained region. It can not save itself by any anti-Yankee fight for sectional interests. There are other bonds of group unity than the bonds of sectionalism, and, likewise, other forces of cleavage. Society has been divided by classes as well as by regions. The South fought in the sixties for class lines as much as for sectional autonomy. The economic landscape is tending to be flattened out by the operations of high finance, industrial expansion, rapid transportation and communication, applied science, and widespread organization. The forces cutting across regionalism or sectionalism do not threaten. They operate. No region of the United States has a monopoly of debtors or creditors, of paupers or plutocrats, of radicals or conservatives. There are rich men in the poverty-stricken South and poor men in the wealthy North. Today an employer of Atlanta may have more in common with an employer of Boston than with an employee of Atlanta. Millionaires of Houston may feel closer to millionaires of New York than to proletarians of their home city. Armies of unemployed tend to develop a keener sense of class than of region.

The South will continue to be different in certain physical respects. The river system and the Appalachian mountains will not disappear under the influence of economic change. Geography as well as the universe must be accepted. Climate, rainfall, swamps, and hills will continue to influence the character and tempo of Southern society, though engineering, sanitation, and air-conditioning may reduce the effect of these physical factors. As air-conditioning expands in my direction, I have little regret over giving up a regional "90 in the shade."

It is important to recognize that regional planning must be limited and guided by national policy. The tenant problem of the South is a community, regional, and national question. Only the nation, not the South alone, can solve the inadequacies and inequalities of the cotton economy, and the nation must take account of the world aspects of the problem. The Negro problem, in its economic aspects and otherwise, is becoming comparatively less Southern and more national.

FORTY ACRES AND STEEL MULES

The incidence of the national economy of scarcity has fallen heavily on the South. Not only tariff protection, but the whole centralized control of industrial production has denied consumers, including Southern consumers, a fair share of the fruits of technological development, of the increased and improved productive capacity. This lack of balance between production and consumption was clearly revealed by the recent exhaustive studies of the Brookings Institution on the actual workings and capacities of the American capitalistic system. Many a Southern farmer appreciates the significance of this imbalance without reading these learned studies. As the most predominantly agricultural area of the country, the South has an unusually large number of producers who are victims of high prices for consumer goods which they buy and of low prices for the goods which they sell for the world market. The Roosevelt administration's policy of granting benefit payments to farmers tends somewhat artificially to correct the discrimination against them. But this policy may be precarious, and it points toward a relative scarcity rather than toward an abundance of production and consumption. Crop control seeks to use the weapon of scarcity, though soil improvement programs inevitably point toward more agricultural capacity and more farm products sooner or later.

The South would have much to gain in championing a national policy based on a chart of plenty, with emphasis on consumers' interest. In spite of the lag in the march of time in Dixie, this region can not and should not escape further industrialization and further agricultural mechanization. Industrially the backward South might skip a generation and move ahead of the rest of the country, or catch up with it, through an increase in both production and consumption, which many experts and reformers have indicated as possible and desirable for America. It should be possible, in thought and in action, to differentiate between industry and certain profit-seeking business practices which have fed upon both industry and agriculture, upon some of the most backward types of industry and agriculture. We have been witnessing a generation of slavery to machines and their owners. We may be approaching an era in which machines become the slaves of society without heavy tolls to privileged owners and entre-

THE SOUTH'S ROLE IN THE NATION

preneurs. Such an era should intuitively appeal to leisure-loving Southerners. The South has known human slavery. Why should it not know and appreciate mechanical slaves? With machines for the slaves of a democracy, we may be enabled to release our minds from concern over economic production or income and to indulge in the non-economic activities and contemplations of life, just as did a few privileged Southerners in the eighteen-fifties.

But pending the arrival of an economy of abundance and an accompanying renaissance, it behooves the South and Southerners to be concerned with an immediate improvement of the region's low production and income status. It is pertinent to note that the ills of the South are the ills of class more than of region or section. The South, with its low per capita wealth, high birth rate, and high illiteracy, is both a victim and an agent of economic exploitation. It is too easy and too simple to charge the ills of the South up to extra-regional control. It is more to the point to say that the South has disproportionately large numbers of the three overlapping groups of Americans who have been most consistently exploited by the "American system." These three overlapping groups are farmers, including tenant farmers; laborers, including unorganized laborers; and Negroes, including many farmers, especially tenant farmers, and laborers.

The South has about half of the farmers of the United States and more than half of the tenant farmers. It has been observed that Southern cotton farmers add a billion dollars annually to the wealth of the world and remain in comparative poverty. As the economic dice have been loaded against the farmers, they have been loaded against the South, with many Southerners participating in the winnings.

The South has a greater proportion of common and unorganized laborers than any other equal area of the country. The wage differential against Southern labor applies particularly to unorganized labor. As the economic dice have been loaded against laborers, they have been loaded against the South, with many Southerners participating in the winnings.

The South contains about two thirds of the twelve million Negroes in the United States. As the economic dice have been loaded against the

FORTY ACRES AND STEEL MULES

Negroes (and how they have been!), they have been loaded against the South, with many Southerners participating in the winnings.

The South will itself never escape exploitation until an end is put to the exploitation of farmers, laborers, and Negroes. The South will never have economic security until these groups of Americans have economic security. The South will never be highly productive until these groups are highly productive. The South will never have its share of the national income until these groups have their share of the national income. The South will never be an educated democracy until these groups are educated and have democracy. The limitations on these classes are limitations on Southern communities and civilization.

It is futile to look for much good in Southern regionalism or sectionalism or to talk against extra-regional control as long as these major groups are held down. We can not wait for long-range planning or for more difficult long-range action. We have a regional disadvantage, which we can partly remove by an avowed championship, in the nation, of the need of farmers, laborers, and Negroes for a larger share of the national income. The South owes it to itself to aid its own farmers, including tenant farmers, and its own laborers, including common laborers, by demanding a better deal for all farmers and all laborers everywhere. Promoting the social interest of these classes is the best regional policy for the South. There can be no inter-regional justice without inter-class justice. The square deal for classes, including the numerous working classes, will prevent a raw deal for the region. It will furnish the most effective answer to the problem of demagoguery, which so frequently bobs up in the cotton country and which thrives on a regional and a class sense of exploitation. The composition of class conflict will go far toward composing regional conflict. Whether the South is to present a final picture of disintegration or of stability depends on whether the South dodges or solves its farmer-labor problems.

SELECTED BIBLIOGRAPHY

The principal works cited or quoted in the previous pages are included in this list.

Ashley, A. W., "Farm Tenancy" in *Encyclopaedia of the Social Sciences*, Vol. VI. New York, 1931.

Barker, T. D., *Libraries of the South*. Chicago, 1936.

Brunner, E. de S., and Kolb, J. H., *Rural Social Trends*. New York, 1933.

Childs, M. W., *Sweden: The Middle Way*. New Haven, 1936.

Cohn, David I., *Picking America's Pockets*. New York, 1936.

Commission on Interracial Co-operation, *The South's Landless Farmers*. Atlanta, 1937.

Couch, W. T. (editor), *Culture in the South*. Chapel Hill, 1934. This book contains a chapter by A. N. J. Den Hollander on "The Tradition of the 'Poor Whites.'"

Dollard, John, *Caste and Class in a Southern Town*. New Haven, 1937. Appendix i of this book is an essay by Leonard W. Doob on "Poor Whites: A Frustrated Class."

Eddy, Sherwood, *A Door of Opportunity*. New York, 1937.

Elliott, Howard, Roper, Daniel C., and Soule, George, *Report of the Special Committee on Reclamation and Rural Development*. Department of the Interior, Bureau of Reclamation, Washington, 1927.

Gide, Charles, *Communist and Coöperative Colonies* (translated by E. F. Rowe). New York, 1930.

Heer, Clarence, *Income and Wages in the South*. Chapel Hill, 1930.

Hoffsommer, Harold, *Landlord-Tenant Relations and Relief in Alabama*. Federal Emergency Relief Administration, Research Bulletin, Ser. 11, No. 9. Washington, 1935.

Howe, F. C., *Denmark: The Coöperative Way*. New York, 1936.

Johnson, Charles S., Embree, Edwin R., and Alexander, W. W., *The Collapse of Cotton Tenancy*. Chapel Hill, 1935.

Johnson, Gerald, *The Wasted Land*. Chapel Hill, 1937.

SELECTED BIBLIOGRAPHY

KESTER, Howard, *Revolt Among the Sharecroppers*. New York, 1936.

LITTLE, Clifton T., *Restless Americans*. Public Affairs Pamphlets, No. 9. Washington, 1936.

MEAD, Elwood, *Helping Men Own Farms*. New York, 1920.

MOLYNEAUX, Peter, *The Cotton South and American Trade Policy*. World Affairs Book No. 17. New York, 1936.

National Resources Committee, *Farm Tenancy*. Report of the President's Committee. Washington, 1937.

———, *Regional Factors in National Planning*. Washington, 1935.

ODUM, Howard W., *Southern Regions*. Chapel Hill, 1936.

OWSLEY, Frank L., "The Pillars of Agrarianism," *The American Review*, IV (March, 1935), 529-547.

RAPER, A. F., *Preface to Peasantry*. Chapel Hill, 1936.

RHYNE, J. J., *Some Southern Cotton Mill Workers and Their Villages*. Chapel Hill, 1930.

RICHARDS, H. I., *Cotton and the AAA*. Washington, 1936.

Southern Forest Experiment Station, *Forest Survey Releases*. New Orleans, 1934.

———, *Occasional Papers*. New Orleans, 1934.

Southern Policy Papers. Nos. 1-10. Issued by the Southern Policy Committee. Chapel Hill, 1936-37.

Southern Regional Committee of the Social Science Research Council, *Problems of the Cotton Economy*. Dallas, 1936.

TANNENBAUM, Frank, *Darker Phases of the South*. New York, 1924.

TERPENNING, Walter A., *Village and Open-Country Neighborhoods*. New York, 1931.

THOMAS, Norman, *The Plight of the Share-Cropper*. New York, 1934.

TURNER, H. A., *A Graphic Summary of Farm Tenure*. United States Department of Agriculture, Miscellaneous Publication No. 261. Washington, 1936.

Twelve Southerners, *I'll Take My Stand*. New York, 1930.

United States Department of Agriculture, Farm Security Administration (formerly Resettlement Administration), *Land Policy Circular*. Washington, monthly.

United States Senate, *Hearing before a Subcommittee of the Committee on Agriculture and Forestry, 74th Congress, 1st Session on S. 1800*. Washington, 1935.

VANCE, Rupert B., *Human Geography of the South*. Chapel Hill, 1932.

———, *Regional Reconstruction: A Way Out for the South*. Chapel Hill, 1935.

———, *The South's Place in the Nation*. Public Affairs Pamphlets, No. 6. Washington, 1936.

WILSON, L. R., and WIGHT, E. A., *County Library Service in the South*. Chicago, 1935.

WOODSON, C. G., *The Rural Negro*. Washington, 1930.

WOOFTER, T. J., Jr., *Landlord and Tenant on the Cotton Plantation*. Works Progress Administration, Division of Social Research, Research Monograph V. Washington, 1936.

———, "The Tennessee Valley Regional Plan." *Social Forces*, XII (March, 1934), 329-339.